The CIVIL WAR HISTORY Series

# FLORIDA
## IN THE CIVIL WAR

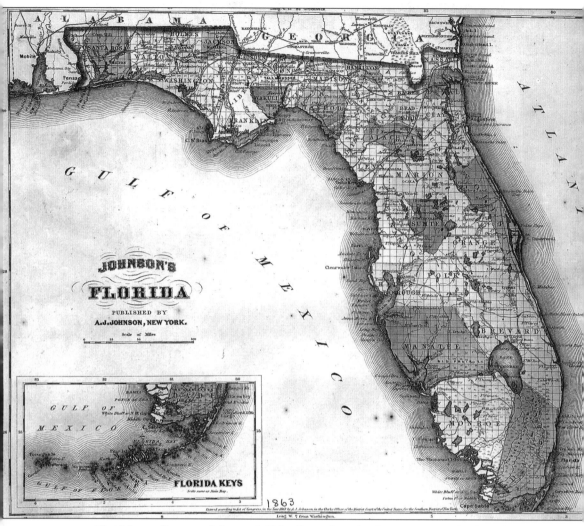

Florida's coastline extended some 1,400 miles and much of it was not populated. Enforcing the blockade was difficult and dangerous for Union forces. (Tebeau–Field Library of Florida History.)

THE **CIVIL WAR HISTORY** SERIES

# FLORIDA
## IN THE CIVIL WAR

**LEWIS N. WYNNE AND ROBERT A. TAYLOR**

ARCADIA

ISBN 0-7385-1368-7

Published by Arcadia Publishing,
an imprint of Tempus Publishing, Inc.
2 Cumberland Street
Charleston, SC 29401

Printed in Great Britain.

Library of Congress Catalog Card Number: 2001093947

For all general information contact Arcadia Publishing at:
Telephone 843-853-2070
Fax 843-853-0044
E-Mail sales@arcadiapublishing.com

For customer service and orders:
Toll-Free 1-888-313-2665

Visit us on the Internet at http://www.arcadiapublishing.com

*This book is dedicated to my children, Patrick and Lisa,
and to my ever-tolerant wife, Debra.
I would also like to dedicate this work to my mother, Lola M. Wynne,
and my father-in-law, Herman Chapin.*

—Nick Wynne

*As always, this is dedicated to my wife, Virginia Taylor, as well as to our parents.
The support of the Florida Institute of Technology is also appreciated. And special
thanks to Paul and Joanne Dair for services above and beyond the call of duty.*

—Robert A. Taylor

# CONTENTS

# PREFACE

It is our intention to provide the reader with a pictorial and general overview of Florida in the Civil War. We have sacrificed footnotes in favor of readability, but we hope the more serious scholar will benefit from the extensive bibliography we have included to discover more detailed information. We have drawn on a number of published sources for the text of this book, and while we have avoided the tedium of footnotes, we have included an extensive list of secondary sources for further reading. In addition, we have culled approximately 130 pictures from various collections to illustrate this volume. We hope that providing a visual accompaniment the reader will be able to fully grasp the texture of Florida society and to understand the experiences of all Floridians during this period.

As is the case for all honest authors, many people need to be thanked for their support, assistance, and encouragement. Without them, this project would have taken a lot more time and effort. The authors would like to extend our thanks to the volunteer staff of the Tebeau-Field Library of Florida History in Cocoa, Florida, for all they did—individually and collectively to assist us.

Robert A. Taylor
Nick Wynne

# 1. SEVEN DAYS OF DESTINY

On January 10, 1861, just two months shy of its 16th anniversary as a state, Florida became the third state to secede from the Union. The decision to follow the lead of South Carolina and Mississippi in severing the bonds of the Federal union came after four decades of rancorous bickering between political leaders in the state over the changing currents of national politics and the increasingly fractious dispute over slavery, state rights, and industrialization. Although there were many ties that bound Floridians to the Union, the relative youth of the state as a member of the larger nation meant that many of these restraints, newly made and weak, were still easily broken. Within the state, serious political and social divisions were evident. Most of the disputes that wracked the nation were played out in the microcosm of Florida politics.

While Florida was perceived of as a solid plantation-slave state, thousands of yeomen farmers and cattlemen had moved into the peninsula, lured by the free lands offered by the Armed Occupation Act and filled with notions of riches to be made on the frontier. Relegated to the coasts of the state and to the broad hammock-filled plains of the south central area, these "Crackers" led a hardscrabble existence of subsistence farming and cattle ranching. Land alone was not a solid foundation for achieving easy wealth, nor could dreams of success be successfully realized without wealth or powerful connections to begin with. While a few unusual individuals did achieve great things, the majority of the yeomen found life in Florida a day-to-day struggle to survive. With the diminution of their hopes and aspirations came a growing resentment against those who lived the Southern dream of vast plantations, large mansions, and numerous slaves.

The inhabitants of East and West Florida, heirs to the legacy of Spanish and British occupation and for many years the dominant political force in Florida, constituted another sizeable group of independent-minded citizens. For them, the upstart planters, who claimed north and central Florida as their own and made it into a replica of other Southern states, were parvenus of the worst sort. The smoldering resentments of these citizens over their loss of importance and influence in Florida affairs placed many of them squarely in opposition to the desires of the planting class.

*Scrub cattle, descendants of the herds brought in by the Spanish, provided the lower classes of whites in Florida sustenance and some annual income. (Jacksonville Historical Society.)*

*Gamble Mansion, now a state historic site, was typical of the antebellum homes of many of Florida's planter elites. (Florida State Archives.)*

8

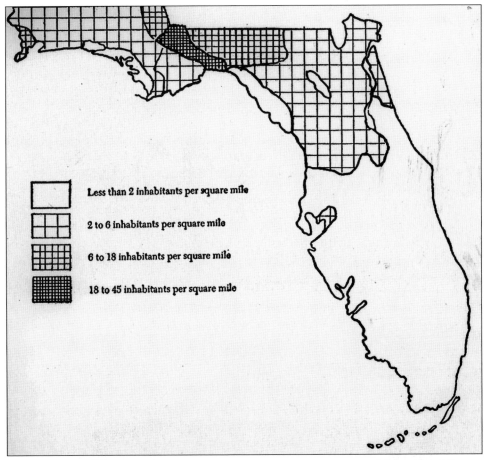

*In 1860, most Floridians lived in the northern and central parts of the state. The heavily settled areas around Tallahassee represented the heart of the state's plantation belt. (From Abbey,* Florida: Land of Change.*)*

In November 1860, when the Florida legislature voted for a Secession Convention to be held on January 3, 1861, opposition to the measure was strong, but not strong enough to stop it from being approved. Even more important to later events was the failure of the pro-Union, anti-secession delegates to muster enough votes to force the Convention to submit its decision to a popular vote. Dominated by planters and their allies, the legislature placed the decision on secession squarely in the hands of the Convention delegates, who answered neither to the legislature nor to the people.

Those who made the decision to make Florida an independent nation until such time as it could join a confederation of like-minded Southern states were not typical of the population of Florida in 1861. By virtue of wealth, education, and political experience, the delegates to the Secession Convention, in the main, were members of the planter class, slaveholders who operated large plantations given to the production of large cash crops, such as cotton and sugar. Concentrated in north and central Florida, these men had close social, political, and economic ties to leaders in the older states of the South. Indeed, many of these men were from prominent planting families in the Carolinas, Georgia, Alabama, and Mississippi. Slavery and the protection of slavery were of paramount importance to them, and few were willing to tolerate any individual or group that threatened this institution. Eighty-four percent (58) of the 62 delegates who voted for immediate secession were slave owners, while 5 of the 7 who voted against the adoption of the ordinance owned slaves.

Of Florida's 1860 population of 140,424 persons, slaves constituted nearly 44 percent. Of the 77,746 whites that appeared in the 1860 Census, only 5,152 were slave owners. This small group, a mere 3.6 percent of the white population, also controlled 71 percent of the cash value of all farm property in the state in 1860, which was concentrated in seven plantation counties in Middle Florida. Because of the constitutional requirement to count slaves as "three-fifths" of a person for voting purposes, this seven-county region also enjoyed a considerable and disproportionate representation in the Florida legislature. Throughout the 15 years of statehood, planters or their allies had controlled the statehouse and governor's office. They carried this unbalanced political power with them to the Secession Convention.

*While many planters lived in splendid mansions, the majority of Florida's yeomen lived in crude log cabins such as this one. (Florida State Archives.)*

LEFT: *Richard Keith Call, former territorial governor and friend of Andrew Jackson, was a staunch opponent of secession. (Tebeau-Field Library of Florida History.)*
RIGHT: *Edmund Ruffin of Virginia was an ardent secessionist whose appearance before the Florida Secession Convention spurred delegates to leave the Union. (National Archives.)*

Yet Floridians did not universally approve the action of the Convention. Birthed in 1821 by Andrew Jackson, who, as president in 1832, was willing to take the nation to war to preserve the Union, Florida was a microcosm of the various political ideas and economic divisions that appeared in all Southern states. Fully 96 percent of the state's population were not slave owners, but were engaged in small farming, cattle ranching, timbering, day laboring, manufacturing, and mercantilism or in professional pursuits. While many of these individuals had direct or indirect ties with planters, the vast majority of the population had few connections to them. Just as the older plantation states experienced clear class divisions between planters, yeomen farmers, and urban residents, Florida experienced the same separations and conflicts. For these small farmers and urban dwellers, secession had little appeal—a fact that would surface as pro-Union activity when war came.

Opposition to secession, however, was not limited to non-planters. Some men, such as Richard Keith Call, a former territorial governor and intimate of Jackson, labeled secession as treason and wanted nothing to do with it. Others, such as David S. Walker and George T. Ward, urged caution and compromise. These were the same men who had been able to diffuse the ardor of the secessionists during the Nullification Crisis of 1832 and the sectional controversies of 1850. Still others, such as David Levy Yulee and Stephen

LEFT: *U.S. Senator David Levy Yulee accepted the decision of his fellow Floridians to leave the Union. (Tebeau-Field Library of Florida History.)*
RIGHT: *Florida's other senator, Stephen R. Mallory of Pensacola, served as the secretary of the navy for the newly formed Confederate States of America. (Artwork by Jeanette Boughner.)*

R. Mallory, were reluctant secessionists at best, opposed to separation, but clearly willing to abide by the decision of the state convention. Despite their political power and personal prestige, these men and their supporters were unable to frustrate the secession-minded planters. Their calls for caution and compromise were for naught as Convention delegates fell under the sway of prominent Southern nationalists like E.C. Bullock of Alabama, L.S. Spratt of South Carolina, and Edmund Ruffin of Virginia, who came to Tallahassee to urge immediate action. Most delegates to the Convention listened attentively to these calls, since many of them were bound by family and business ties to planters in those states.

Outside the Convention, state officials moved to counter real or imagined efforts by the Federal government to maintain control of the situation. Newspapers reported Federal troop movements in Southern states, while in Washington, Senators David Levy Yulee and Stephen R. Mallory used their official standing to secure additional information from Southern sympathizers in the War Department. Each new revelation brought additional pressure on Convention delegates to act swiftly.

Even as delegates debated, Governor Madison Starke Perry, alarmed at the news that Federal troops were on their way to reinforce critical forts and to destroy national arsenals in the state, sent state militia units to seize these installations before they could be emptied or destroyed. The Quincy Guards took control of the Chattahoochee Arsenal, with its large supply of powder and shot, on January 5. On January 7, the single Federal soldier guarding Fort Marion in St. Augustine surrendered the facility to local volunteers; while on January 8, Fort Clinch on Amelia Island was occupied by Florida troops. Although

*Governor Perry received this telegram from Georgia Governor Joseph E. Brown just a few days before Florida seceded. Brown assured Perry that Georgia would secede soon. More importantly, Brown wondered, "Has Florida occupied the Forts?" (Tebeau-Field Library of Florida History.)*

these fortifications were thought to be important, they could not compare to those held by Federal troops in Pensacola.

In Pensacola, Lieutenant Adam Slemmer of the U.S. First Artillery, commander of the Pensacola forts, began his preparations to deny control of the Federal forts in the area to any outside power. Although his force of 81 men was woefully inadequate for the task, Slemmer decided that his best hope of maintaining control of the port was by concentrating his forces in Fort Pickens on nearby Santa Rosa Island. This fort, in poor condition and cut off from the mainland, nevertheless commanded the mouth of Pensacola Bay. Although this tactic meant abandoning several smaller forts on the mainland and the important facilities at the Pensacola Navy Yard, control of Fort Pickens would mean control of Florida's most important harbor. On the night of January 10, he completed his movement to Pickens. Federal troops would hold this fort for the next five years.

When it became apparent that nothing could stop the secessionists, many of the men who had been the most vocal in arguing against secession abandoned their opposition and quickly moved into leadership positions in the Confederate national government. Having given their best efforts, they subscribed to the philosophy of "My state, right or wrong, but my state!" Some—but not all. Former governor Richard Keith Call called secession treason and made his opinions public when he confronted a jubilant crowd on the steps of his Tallahassee home. Still others, such as Ossian Bingley Hart of Jacksonville and William Marvin of Key West, remained quietly "unionist" in their opinions, eventually enjoying the protection of the Federal troops that occupied these towns.

On January 10, 1861, Floridians were thrust into a maelstrom that would not subside for decades. For them, the decision made by a few wealthy planters would severely impact their lives for generations. Despite their lack of input into the decision-making process,

*Built by the Spanish, the Castillo de San Marcos had been rechristened Fort Marion. In 1861, it was garrisoned by a small Federal unit that quickly surrendered to troops of the Florida militia. (National Archives.)*

*Fort Clinch, which stood at the mouth of Fernandina's harbor, was quickly occupied by Florida troops. (Contemporary drawing; Florida State Archives.)*

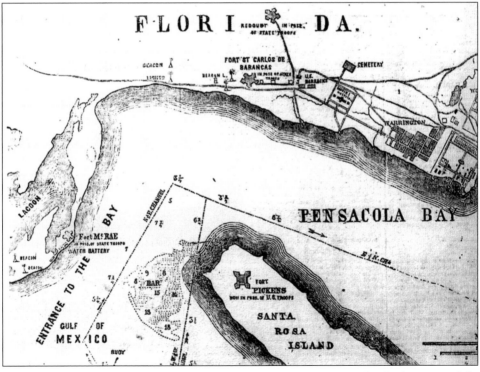

*This February 1861 drawing from* Leslie's Illustrated Newspaper *graphically demonstrated the commanding position of Fort Pickens in Pensacola.*

LEFT: *Ossian Bingley Hart, a Jacksonville Unionist, was an outspoken opponent of secession in 1861. He became a Republican governor of Florida in the immediate post-war period. (Florida State Archives.)* RIGHT: *Although more muted in his opposition to secession, William Marvin, a resident of Key West, was a Unionist who also served as a post-war governor of Florida. (Florida State Archives.)*

the majority of white Floridians embraced the results. When the announcement was made that the Ordinance of Secession had been approved and signed, dancing and wild celebrations broke out in the streets of Tallahassee. Of the state's white population of 77,000, approximately 15,000 served in the Confederate military services, and of these, some 5,000 were killed. An additional number of Floridians, white and black, served in units of the Federal military.

At home, Floridians suffered the same deprivations and hardships that their fellow Confederates in other states experienced. And while Florida escaped the wholesale destruction that some other states endured, it was subjected to invasion by Federal armies, blockade by the United States Navy, and loss of economic stability. The war was the impetus that brought Florida solidly in the ranks of Southern states and, in no small way, marked the end of its frontier existence.

## 2. THE WAR BEGINS

The presidential election of 1860 spawned the greatest challenge ever faced by the young United States. When Americans went to the polls the disruptive issues of the past decade clearly weighed on their minds and influenced their votes. The citizens of Florida, a state only since 1845, were not immune to this political fervor. The debate over chattel slavery and its expansion westward had wrecked the Whig Party, split the Democratic Party into hostile Northern and Southern wings, and finally caused the creation of the new Republican Party. The notion of a "black Republican" winning the White House and then using the power of the Federal government to destroy the institution of slavery was nightmarish to most Floridians and their fellow Southerners.

When the ballots were tabulated in that fateful November, Florida's electoral votes went to Southern Democrat John C. Breckinridge of Kentucky. However, a surprising number of voters opted for John Bell and the more moderate Constitutional Union Party. Republican Abraham Lincoln received no votes in Florida, as his name did not appear on the ballot. It is doubtful that he would have garnered many Florida votes had this not been the case. In spite of this, Lincoln went on to win the presidential race without Florida and the South due to victories in electoral-rich states in the North. What little Floridians knew about the president-elect they did not like, and they were convinced that he was nothing more than an abolitionist bent on destroying the Southern way of life.

Lincoln's election galvanized the Southern states and calls for drastic action filled the air. At the urging of Florida governor Madison Starke Perry, the state legislature in late November 1861 issued a call for a special convention to consider the question of whether Florida should remain in the Union under the circumstances. Most Floridians did not question whether Florida should opt for secession and independence, only how and when such a step should be taken. The thought that separation might not be peaceful was on the Perry's mind when he also requested funds from the legislature for weapons and military equipment for state troops that might be called to service in defend the state from the "Lincolnites." The necessity of preparations became more apparent when South Carolina issued an ordinance of session and cut its ties to the United States on December 20.

*John C. Breckinridge of Kentucky won all of Florida's electoral votes in the presidential election of 1860. (*Leslie's Illustrated Newspaper.*)*

Florida citizens who championed immediate secession, called "fire-eaters," were thrilled with the Carolinians' bold move and hoped their state would quickly act likewise. Others wanted to wait for the situation to develop further before taking the secession plunge but agreed that Florida had no place in a Union hostile to slavery. Such "cooperationists" wanted the Southern states to act as one solid unit when challenging the Federal government. A small anti-secession Union element also existed inside Florida, but it was swept aside by the emotion of the moment and the swift response of the "fire-eaters." Floridians again went to their polling places and selected delegates for the state secession convention on December 22.

Those chosen to participate made their way to Tallahassee to begin their important deliberations scheduled to begin on January 3, 1861. Of the 69 delegates who attended few doubted that secession was a valid and legal means for a people who believed that their rights were in danger from what appeared to be a tyrannical national government. An anxious crowd gathered in the state capitol to watch the proceedings and included several representatives from other Southern states contemplating the same action like fiery Edmund Ruffin of Virginia. All such visitors urged swift and vigorous action to help begin what they truly believed to be the beginning of the second American Revolution. Governor Perry heartily agreed with these sentiments and pressed the delegates to draft an ordinance of secession for Florida without delay.

Events outside Tallahassee also influenced the delegates as they pondered the right strategy. Local militia units moved in early January to seize control of all Federal property in the state. The U.S. government arsenals at Apalachicola and Chattahoochee were taken without resistance, and their considerable stores of ammunition boosted Florida's limited supply. Fort Clinch near Fernandina likewise surrendered to state forces without incident, as did the Castillo de San Marcos, now named Fort Marion, in St. Augustine. These installations fell so easily because they were greatly under-manned and had received no clear orders from the War Department in far off Washington as to what they should do in this extraordinary situation. No one wanted to be the first to spark violence and bloodshed that might touch off a bloody civil war.

On January 7, 1861, the secession convention voted that Florida should legally resign from the United States and draft a secession ordinance to do just that. Some members attempted to delay anything further until neighboring states Georgia and Alabama had made their positions on the grave issue clear. Mississippi followed South Carolina out of the Union on January 9, which only fueled the cause of immediate secessionists. At roughly 10 a.m. on the morning of January 10, the secession convention delegates filed into the capitol to cast their vote on Florida's future. In the end secession carried the day with 62 members voting "yes" and only 5 delegates voting "no." The die had indeed been cast.

Not all Floridians approved of this action, as the five "no" votes indicated. When members of the convention gathered to sign the final secession ordinance on the east portico of the capitol building only 64 out of the 69 showed up. One brave Unionist dared to speak his mind on the action the gathering had taken. Former territorial governor Richard Keith Call, one of the founding fathers of Florida statehood, angrily cried that the delegates had "opened the gates of Hell, from which shall flow the curses of the damned which shall sink you to perdition!" Only later when the suffering of civil war was a hard fact would Floridians see these prophetic words as true.

*These are the outer gates of Fort Marion in St. Augustine. (Library of Congress.)*

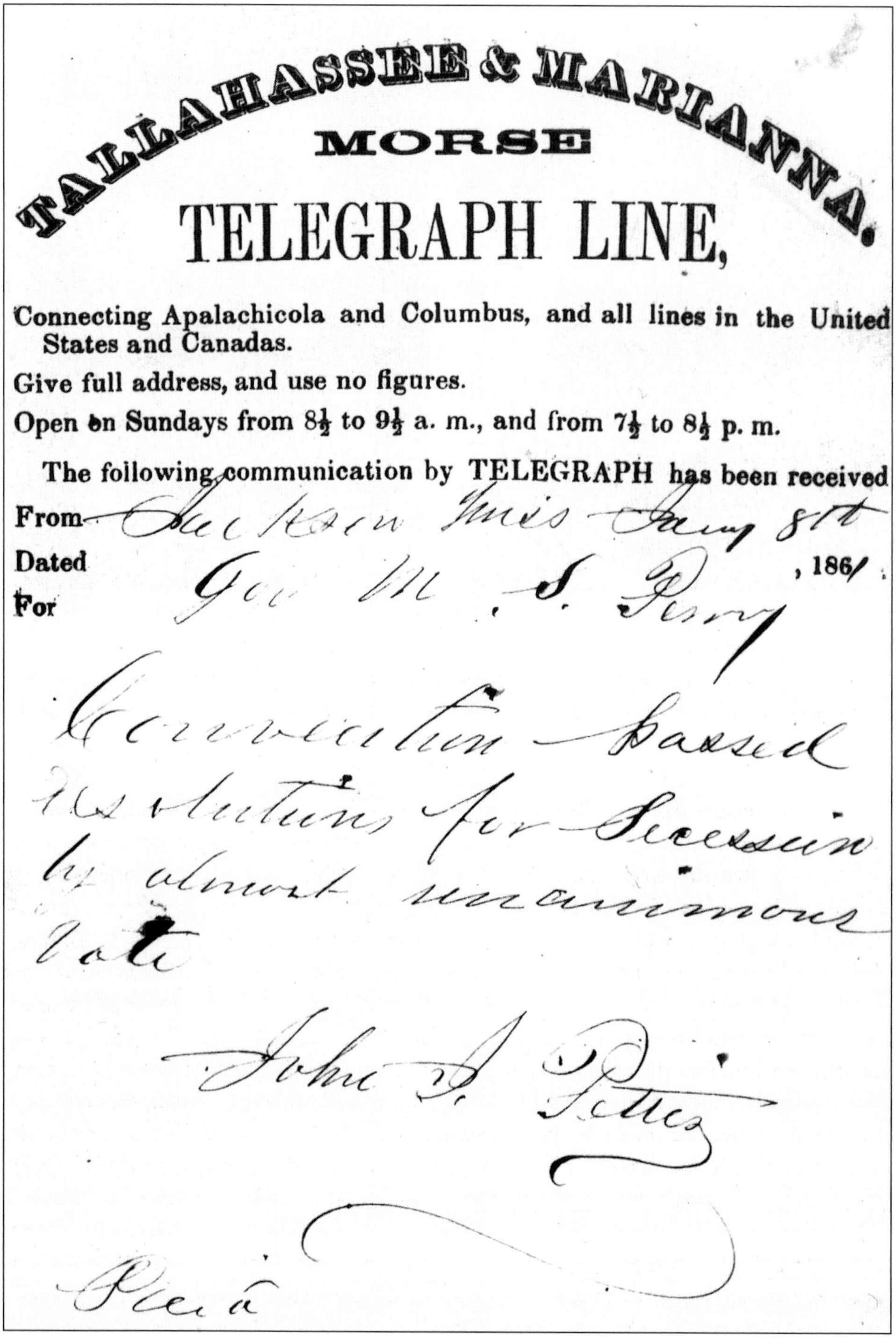

## TALLAHASSEE & MARIANNA.

### MORSE

# TELEGRAPH LINE,

Connecting Apalachicola and Columbus, and all lines in the United
  States and Canadas.

Give full address, and use no figures.

Open on Sundays from 8½ to 9½ a. m., and from 7½ to 8½ p. m.

  The following communication by TELEGRAPH has been received

From *Jackson Miss Jany 8th*

Dated _____ , 186*1*

For *Gov M. S. Perry*

*Convention passed
Resolutions for Secession
by almost unanimous
vote*

*John J. Pettus*

*Pres.ᵗ*

*While Florida's Secession Convention was going through with its decision to take the state out of the Union, Governor Perry received the news that Mississippi had become the second Southern state to secede.*

LEFT: *Jefferson Davis, a former U.S. senator from Mississippi, was elected the provisional president of the new Confederate States of America.*

RIGHT: *Alexander H. Stephens, an irascible social misfit, was elected vice-president of the Confederacy. Stephens spent much of his time fighting with Davis in Richmond or at home in Georgia.*

After the January 10 vote, Florida became, at least in its eyes, an independent country. The people of the state were never given the chance to vote on secession themselves, but few doubted that the ordinance would have passed with a solid majority supporting it. Why did the people of Florida take and sustain such a momentous step? Large numbers of South Carolinians had moved southward to Florida in the 1850s in search of cheap lands and brought their political philosophies with them. Also, over 80 percent of the members of the secession convention were slaveholders, which could not help but color their view of Florida's options under the Lincoln Administration. Though the vast majority of white Florida residents were small yeoman farmers and not plantation owners, they dreamed of the day they could move up into that class, and for them, the only way to make that move was on the backs of African slaves who were essential for success in the antebellum South. Any move by the Federal government to take away the ladder to their version of the American dream, real or feared, was reason enough to cut the ties of Union.

The majority of the white populace welcomed the news of Florida's independence and several communities saw parades and other joyous demonstrations. Those with doubts for the most part kept them to themselves. None of the celebrants imagined that this action might lead to a civil war that would cost untold amounts of treasure and blood. Any who thought the North might respond with force were sure that such a war would be settled in one or two battles that the South would easily win. Events in the early months of 1861 seemed to support that view.

Before the end of spring seven lower Southern states had seceded and began making serious plans to form a new national government. Northerners looked on in stunned disbelief as representatives from these newly independent states made their way to Montgomery, Alabama. A three-man Florida delegation, consisting of James Patton Anderson, Jackson Morton, and James Owens, took their seats at the historic convention. In a scant few weeks their labors produced a Confederate constitution, a provisional congress, and provisional executive leaders in Mississippi's Jefferson Davis and Georgia's Alexander H. Stephens. While a reluctant president, Davis set to work to fill the executive branch of the new Confederate States of America with capable leaders, and found several from Florida.

For the position of secretary of the Confederate navy, President Davis tapped Floridian Stephen R. Mallory. Mallory had been born on Trinidad, but grew up in Key West and by 1861 was a prominent citizen of Pensacola. After a career as a lawyer and judge, Mallory was elected to the United States Senate, where he chaired the Committee on Naval Affairs. Few knew as much about the workings of the United States Navy as did Mallory, and he seemed the perfect choice to oversee the creation of a Confederate naval force. Events proved this correct, and the Floridian was the only secretary of the navy in a Davis Administration notorious for cabinet member turnover. Mallory labored to find ships and men for a viable navy for the South and advocated the extensive use of steam power and ironclad vessels to be able to overcome the Union fleet's superior numbers.

*Fort Taylor in Key West remained in Federal hands throughout the war.* (Harper's Weekly *and* Florida State Archives.)

*Fort Jefferson was known as the "Gibraltar of the Gulf." Barely finished before the opening of hostilities in 1861, this fortress never experienced a shot fired at it nor did any of its massive guns ever fire in anger. After the war, it served as a prison for Dr. Samuel Mudd. (Tebeau-Field Library of Florida History.)*

As the new rebel government set up shop in Montgomery, Florida went about the business of becoming a Confederate state. Initial moves to seize all Federal property inside the peninsula were for the most part successful, but there were two glaring omissions. Fort Taylor in Key West and Fort Jefferson in the Dry Tortugas remained under United States control and would be so for the duration of the coming war. Fort Taylor formed the center of a soon to be significant Unionist community in one of Florida's largest urban centers. Key West played host to units of the Federal navy engaged in blockading Florida and the rest of the South. Remote Fort Jefferson served as a key element of the Union's military justice system as a very secure prison. It enjoyed the grim reputation as the American Devil's Island and may have helped a few rowdy soldiers maintain discipline out of fear of a tour there.

The other military post that rebel Floridians failed to grasp was the strategically important Fort Pickens. Located on the sandy tip of Santa Rosa Island, the fortification commanded the entrance to Pensacola Bay, one of the South's best anchorages. It also protected a United States Navy Yard filled with supplies and equipment the Confederacy desperately needed. As soon as secession was fact Florida officials in and out of the state pressed that Pickens and the other installations around Pensacola be taken from the Federals without delay. Pensacola's position on the Gulf coast made this imperative enough that neighboring states sent troops to aid in the captures. Smaller Forts Barrancas and McRee were turned over without incident in early February, as would be the navy yard itself. However, Union Lieutenant Adam J. Slemmer, showing considerable initiative for such a junior officer, moved roughly 100 soldiers, sailors, and marines out to isolated Fort Pickens to await orders.

*The Pensacola Navy Yard in Pensacola is pictured here in 1837. (Pensacola Historical Society.)*

Local officials were unhappy that Slemmer had acted in this manner and that he refused to surrender his post without orders from the War Department in Washington. Despite its lack of preparedness and tiny garrison, Yankee-controlled Pickens effectively bottled up the large harbor and posed a real threat to the security of the rest of the Confederate Gulf coast. In time thousands of raw state troops, commanded by the stern Braxton Bragg, would march into Pensacola and train to storm the enemy fort. Bragg, like so many other future generals in both the Union and Confederate armies, had been stationed in Florida during the antebellum years and knew something of the country.

Bragg put his men to building fortifications around Pensacola and learning the hard skills of soldiering under the hot Florida sun. Their situation was not too different from those troops camped around Charleston, South Carolina, waiting for the chance to capture Fort Sumter out in the harbor. Both forts were flashpoints, and an incident at either one could touch off civil war. However, as far as Pickens was concerned, an uneasy truce continued through the spring of 1861. No major actions would take place until the North swore in a new president in March.

Abraham Lincoln made the long journey to Washington and took the oath of office on March 4 and, in a long-awaited speech, told the people of his disunited nation that he would strive to maintain control of all Federal property in the rebel states and regain that which had been illegally taken. Despite this hard line, however, Lincoln did not want to cause the outbreak of open warfare between the sections of the nation if he could avoid it, and certainly was enough of a lawyer to know not to throw the first punch in any potential altercation. The new president probably had never heard of Forts Pickens and Sumter, but these two places would dominate the first weeks and months of his administration.

Cabinet officers gave Lincoln conflicting advice concerning the wisdom of keeping one or more of the forts or abandoning them both. In time he decided to simply re-supply the forts and let the Southerners make the next move.

Jefferson Davis, under pressure from South Carolinians to act on the matter of Fort Sumter, ordered that the garrison there be shelled out of their island bastion. The cannons roared on April 12, 1861, and civil war was no longer a fear but a reality. The final straw and first clash of this internecine struggle could have taken place at the walls of Florida's Fort Pickens, but fate decided otherwise. After some confusing orders, reinforcements began landing on Santa Rosa Island to strengthen the Union's hold on Pickens and Pensacola Bay. This grip would not be removed for the entire war, depriving the South of a potential destination for blockade-runners and creating a troubling Yankee lodgment on the Confederacy's southern coastline.

The firing on Fort Sumter and Lincoln's subsequent call for 75,000 volunteers from the states to put down what he believed to be a rebellion in the South was the catalyst that placed four more states in the Confederate column. Virginia, North Carolina, Tennessee, and Arkansas, heretofore cool toward secession, would not take up arms against their fellow Southerners and instead joined them. Such events forced people to choose between their home states and the Federal government, and in more than a few cases tore families apart. Probably the greatest strain was on the officers of the United States Army and Navy who were Southern born. They had taken an oath to the government of the United States but now were faced with the unpleasant situation of being asked to fight against their families and friends at home. Dozens of regular officers resigned their commissions, thereby throwing away their careers, and went south to join the Confederate cause. Although there were relatively few Floridians serving as officers in the regular army and navy due to Florida's recent admission to the Union, at least two made the fateful choice and went on to high rank and important commands in the growing rebel army.

Edmund Kirby Smith, born in St. Augustine in 1824, graduated from West Point in 1845. The young infantry officer built a solid career on the frontier and as a mathematics instructor at the Academy. Upon learning of Florida's secession Smith resigned his commission in the U.S. Army on March 3, 1861, and offered his services to the Confederacy. Soon wearing a general's star, he served in the western theater and held important commands until 1863 when he was reassigned at own his request. General Smith took on the task of running the vast Trans-Mississippi Department, soon known as "Kirby Smithdom." Here he remained until 1865 when he surrendered his western command and the last Confederate forces still under arms.

The second Floridian to achieve high rank in the rebel army was William Wing Loring. A citizen-soldier, Loring learned the soldier's trade during the Second Seminole War as a volunteer and decided to make the army a career. While no advocate of secession, Loring left the officer corps in May 1861 and soon donned the gray uniform of a Confederate brigadier general. Loring, known as "Old Blizzards," led troops in the Shenandoah Valley, the Vicksburg campaign, and as General John Bell Hood's second-in-command during the disastrous 1864 Tennessee invasion. No stranger to controversy and never comfortable serving under officers whom he had ranked in the "old Army," Loring did give good service to the cause to which he committed himself.

*Edmund Kirby Smith, a native of St. Augustine, was responsible for running the Confederate government and military in the Department of the Trans-Mississippi West after the Federal capture of Vicksburg on July 4, 1863. (Library of Congress.)*

After Fort Sumter both Northern and Southern men rushed to their respective colors and enlisted in what many believed would be a short and glorious contest. Floridians were no exception as men and boys flocked to put their names on enlistment papers that would turn them into infantrymen, cavalrymen, or artillerists. Local companies mustered and marched off to camps of instruction to be formed into battalions and eventually in regiments. Out of a population of 140,000 the state would send roughly 15,000 soldiers to fight for the South, one of the highest percentages of population of any Confederate state. These new recruits, many without uniforms, could never guess that their war would go on for years, carry them far from home, and demand much from them. Most would agree with the notion that the Yankees they were to face were poor fighters who would bolt after the first volley of rifled musket fire. Others never dreamed that they would even have to leave Florida itself to meet the enemy in battle. The illusions these notions bred would soon be swept away by the hard lessons of a real war against a determined foe.

Outfitting such troops proved very expensive, and the Florida state government faced serious financial problems caused by the drain of military spending on the treasury. Newly enrolled units needed weapons, uniforms, shoes, blankets, tents, and all the other supplies necessary to make them into effective combat units. Florida's frontier economy had little in the way of liquid resources to meet this challenge, and soon state leaders worried about how the bills were going to be paid. Neighboring states with more cash might be called upon to help, but such aid could very well have strings attached. As early as February 1861 a newspaper editor suggested that Florida be divided up into three sections with West Florida going to Alabama, cotton-rich Middle Florida joining Georgia, and the remainder of the peninsula left to fend for itself. Wartime pressures quickly put an end to such speculative dreams and halted any expansionist moves against Florida borders.

The problems of finances, military defense, and the presence of Union forces on or near Florida soil fell into the lap of new Governor John Milton when he took the oath of office on October 5, 1861. Milton, a Jackson County planter, proved to be one of the more able state chief executives in the Confederate States. He had no illusions of a quick and easy victory over the Yankees or that Southern independence could be achieved without considerable sacrifice. Milton maintained a good working relationship with President Davis in Richmond, no small feat, and urged other states to cooperate with the new national government for the good of the cause. In the end Milton was a firm advocate of Confederate nationalism and an effective public leader. Unfortunately, by 1865 the pressures of his duties and the South's diminishing chances for victory would overwhelm him.

*Floridians who volunteered for service in state or with Confederate forces were frequently forced to make do without uniforms or government-issued weapons. (Florida State Archives.)*

*This lithograph of pre-war Apalachicola portrays a peaceful little port with two lighthouses. (Florida Publishing Company Photographic Archives.)*

The biggest problem facing the new governor in 1861 was finding the necessary resources to defend Florida's long coastline from Northern attacks. The troops and weapons to do the job did not exist, and those that were in the field faced transfer to more vital areas of the Confederacy. Milton himself wondered why the Federals were taking so long to move against his exposed state and use it as a base to strike at the lower South. However, the Lincoln Administration had as many tribulations as he did, and Union military planners did not place a high priority on returning the peninsula state to Federal control at that point. At times during the war both Washington and Richmond failed to appreciate Florida's strategic value, something Governor Milton never did.

Florida did soon begin to feel Union pressure in 1861 in the form of a naval blockade. The USS *Montgomery* sailed into Apalachicola Bay on June 11, 1861, making the town the first in Florida outside of Pensacola to be cordoned off to maritime traffic. Apalachicola, once one of the state's busiest cotton ports, soon suffered an economic downturn from which it never fully recovered. Farther along the Gulf coast, St. Marks and tiny Tampa joined those harbor communities smothered under Union General Winfield Scott's "Anaconda Plan." Soon practically the whole Florida coastline was under the guns of the U.S. Navy. Only a few brave blockade-runners dared challenge the blockaders by smuggling in badly needed supplies.

Quickly the naval threat to Floridians became a ground one as well. The Federal army and navy realized by mid-1861 that by working together they could create a tremendous amphibious force that could strike almost at will against the rebel shore. The Atlantic and Gulf coasts offered many opportunities to cripple the Confederate war effort and morale and secure bases for further operations at sea and on land. The Confederates could never muster even a fraction of the forces needed to secure its long coastline, stretching as it did from Virginia to Texas. By 1862 rebel authorities began pondering painful decisions about which parts of their country were worthy of allocations of troops and weapons and which sections were expendable. Unfortunately for Florida, the peninsula state did not garner a high ranking. Decisions made in far off Richmond would soon have a major impact on its fate as a Confederate state.

The dawn of 1862 brought little good news to the embattled Confederacy. Union triumphs at Forts Henry and Donelson and the heavy losses at the bloody clash at Shiloh in April created a demand for gray-clad soldiers to shore up the collapsing western theater. Hard decisions had to be made by President Davis and his military advisor, Robert E. Lee, on which areas to strip of defenders. General Lee had already inspected the defenses on the Atlantic coast as far south as Florida and concluded that many of the army units stationed there would be better used elsewhere. The Virginian bluntly informed Governor Milton that the citizens of Florida should take up arms and defend themselves from the Yankee hordes. Where the weapons and military-aged men to create this home defense forces might come from General Lee did not mention.

Under orders, Confederate troops began a general withdrawal from Florida coastal communities and as a result Union forces moved to secure the defenseless towns. In April, Apalachicola and Jacksonville were evacuated and subsequently occupied by the Federals. Jacksonville, near the mouth of the St. Johns River, was destined for several enemy occupations that damaged the town's economy for a time and strained its social fabric. Pensacola was next to go in May, giving the Union blockaders on the Gulf coast a first-rate anchorage and repair facilities that aided in their operations. Residents of these places who did not want to live under Federal authority had little choice but to leave and join the growing ranks of homeless Southerners forced to become refugees.

The relative ease of these occupations, combined with the hopes of finding and supporting loyal Unionist Floridians, spurred the bluecoats to even more missions. The port of Fernandina tempted Union leaders not only for its harbor at the mouth of the

*The military prison in Jacksonville is seen here in 1864. This town, at the mouth of the St. Johns River, was occupied four times during the war. (National Archives.)*

*Federal troops march through Fernandina in 1862. (*New York Illustrated News *and Florida State Archives.)*

St. Marys River, but also its location as the northern terminus of the trans-state Florida Railroad. This line, running across the peninsula to Cedar Key, was a prime military target. Despite Confederate-manned Fort Clinch, very little in the way of defenses protected the town. Locals would often watch from their rooftops the vessels of the Union blockade sailing off their shores and wonder when they would strike. The wait was not long when Northern forces, commanded by Flag Officer Samuel DuPont, landed on Amelia Island and then took the valuable port city on March 4, 1862. Fernandina remained under Union control for the rest of the war.

Florida's oldest city, St. Augustine, would be the next to feel the power of the Union military. Fort Marion, formerly the Castillo de San Marcos, only offered false hope to residents since it was greatly under-manned and lacked modern cannons. As early as September 1861 enemy warships had closed the channel into the city's small harbor and all but ended local commerce. When Union gunboats steamed up the Matanzas River and demanded surrender on March 12, city leaders had few options. They wisely ran up a white flag and accepted defeat without incident. St. Augustine adapted itself to its new reality and managed to enjoy a fairly high standard of living compared to other wartime Florida communities. Stores soon had goods to sell courtesy of captures of blockade-runners by the Union navy, and the town was almost always filled with Union soldiers with money to spend in what, for them, was a very exotic locale. While their blue uniforms were not often welcomed by the pro-Confederates still living within the city gates, their hard currency indeed was.

*St. Augustine, shown here in an 1858 rendering, maintained its tranquil air throughout the war, due primarily to the early and permanent occupation of the town by Federal troops. (National Archives.)*

With a secure foothold on the eastern Florida coastline, Union naval forces soon began pushing up the broad St. Johns to break up communications with the interior of the state and to destroy any property of military value to the rebels. The St. Johns' watery highway into Florida was defended as well as possible by local forces and sharp engagements took place at Yellow and St. Johns Bluffs. However, gunboats became an all-too common sight on the St. Johns and a constant threat to the small flow of smuggled supplies being shuttled across the river from places like Mosquito Inlet on the Atlantic coast for the Confederate government. Also, for African Americans held in bondage in East Florida, these ships soon meant a ticket to freedom. As the war went on a trickle of runaway slaves grew into a steady stream, as these slaves voted with their feet on their desire to escape from servitude in the Confederate states.

Naturally, Floridians were deeply concerned with these seemingly easy Union advances and the capture of so many of the state's urban centers. Fortunately, Federal forces did not have the numbers to push into the interior or to build on their earlier successes, so a stalemate set in. Both sides occasionally would launch small raids and counter-raids against their foes for the better part of two years but this did little to affect the course of the greater war raging to the north. The heart of the state's cotton belt in Middle Florida was for the most part untouched, and slaves continued to labor in the fields. But only the most optimistic could believe that this state of affairs would remain so for very long. With the state stripped of so many of its sons it continued to pose a tempting target, especially since so much of Florida consisted of isolated settlements without roads or certain forms

*Gunboats, such as the USS* Commodore Morris, *patrolled the St. Johns River and fought frequent skirmishes with Confederate troops and artillery batteries. (Florida Publishing Company Photographic Archives.)*

of communication. Also, not all Floridians were enthusiastic supporters of the Confederate cause, and the number of open Unionists in the region would grow as wartime shortages and disruptions made the price of rebellion too high. In time a growing Unionist movement brought all the horrors of a real civil war home to its people.

Confederate government policies did little to heal these growing divisions in early 1862. After considerable debate the Confederate Congress passed the first national conscription law in American history in that year. Military-aged men were now compelled to serve or face harsh consequences. However, the law contained numerous loopholes that allowed the wealthy or the well connected to secure exemptions from the Confederate draft, angering those already shouldering muskets in the ranks. Grumbling about "a rich man's war and a poor man's fight" echoed throughout the South, including Florida. Those evading conscription found many hiding places in the Florida pine prairies and hammocks near Lake Okeechobee. As the war dragged on these draft dodgers and soon outright deserters grew to alarming numbers and threatened isolated settlers. These concerns, coupled with economic troubles, climbing inflation, and lowering standards of living, convinced all the people of Florida that they were indeed now at war.

# 3. ON DISTANT FIELDS
## THE ARMY OF NORTHERN VIRGINIA

With the decision to move the Confederate capital to Richmond, Virginia, Southern strategy was concentrated on protecting the seat of government. Virginia's population (1,596,318) made it the most populous of the Confederate States, accounting for approximately 21 percent of the new nation's total population. Its iron works, arsenals, and shipbuilding centers in Richmond, Harper's Ferry, and Norfolk increased its military importance, particularly for a new nation with only a few such centers.

Confederates were also tied to Virginia from an emotional standpoint as well. Closely associated with the American Revolution and home to many founders of the United States like George Washington, Thomas Jefferson, James Monroe, and James Madison, the state's decision to join the Confederacy gave a sense of legitimacy and continuity to the argument Southerners made that the new nation was a natural and legally constituted development in the American democratic process.

From a military standpoint, the decision to locate the Confederate capital in Richmond had advantages that could be exploited. The well-developed rail, water, and road network in the state allowed for the rapid movement of men and supplies, while the diverse topography provided numerous advantages for both offensive and defensive actions—much more so, as was later proven, for a smaller army with limited resources. The Virginia countryside was fertile and productive, and the large number of small farms could produce enough food and fodder for a sizeable military force. The state's large slave population (490,865) demanded the presence of a large military garrison in the face of hostilities with the Union, and it made sense to have the largest Confederate army stationed there. Finally, Virginia abutted the Federal capital at Washington and offered Confederate authorities with an always-inviting target.

Of course, there were significant disadvantages to the selection of Richmond as the capital of the new Southern nation. First, a considerable number of Virginians disagreed with secession and very early on declared themselves in opposition to the Confederacy. As a result, Virginia was forced to deal with the question of secession itself as the residents of the western mountainous portion of the state seceded and created the new state of West

LEFT: *Joseph Eggleston Johnston, the Confederate commander at Bull Run-Manassas, eventually commanded the Confederate Army of Tennessee in its struggle against Sherman's invasion of Georgia.* RIGHT: *Pierre Gustav Toutant Beauregard, a native of Louisiana, was a Confederate general who commanded forces in a number of different theaters during his Civil War career.*

Virginia, which was quickly recognized by the United States Congress. Second, despite its resources and population, Virginia was geographically a "thumb" that protruded from the Confederacy into the side of the Union. Strong and concerted action against Kentucky and North Carolina by the Federal military would sever it from the rest of the new nation. Fortunately for the Confederacy, this option was never fully exploited by the Union. Third, the long distance from the "Deep" South to the new capital made communications difficult between the various states and armies. The same difficulty existed when, in the later course of the war, troops and supplies from all over the Confederacy were sent to Virginia. Not all Southern states enjoyed the same highly developed transportation network as Virginia. Finally, the same proximity of the Confederate capital to the Union capital that attracted the attention of Confederate strategists also appealed to Federal military planners.

For the Union, the decision to make Richmond the Confederate capital also forced military planners to alter their immediate plans. Richmond seemed like a ripe plum ready for picking, an easy prize to be taken by bold action. The key to a quick Union victory and a definitive end to the Confederate experiment in independence seemed to be the rapid capture of Richmond. On April 15, 1861, newly inaugurated Federal President Abraham Lincoln called for 75,000 volunteers to suppress "combinations too powerful to be suppressed by the ordinary course of judicial proceedings, or by the powers vested in the

Marshals by law." Interestingly, his call for volunteers stressed the necessity to reoccupy Federal properties that had been seized by Confederates but made no mention of the possibility of having to fight an all-out war. Federal officials appeared to regard the newly formed Confederate States of America as an elaborate sham that would collapse after the first major confrontation. Certainly an army of 75,000 volunteers was considered enormous in the context of the times when European armies of 50-60,000 were considered gigantic.

The Confederate response to Lincoln's call for volunteers was to issue its own call. Florida, which had initially been requested to furnish 500 soldiers, saw its troop quota raised to 5,000 over the next six months. Similar requests were made to all the Confederate states. As more and more state troops were moved to Confederate rosters, the Southern forces also began to coalesce into a formidable army. Led by experienced officers, most of whom had served in the old Federal army, and supplied with arms confiscated from former U.S. arsenals or purchased from abroad, Southern troops were rushed to Virginia to defend the Confederate capital from the anticipated Union invasion.

On July 16, a Federal army of 28,500, under the command of Brigadier General Irvin McDowell, pushed out of its encampment at Washington and headed south into Virginia. Confederate forces, led by Brigadier General Joseph E. Johnston and P.G.T. Beauregard

*The much-anticipated "easy" victory at Bull Run-Manassas turned into a rout of the Union army, as this contemporary sketch depicts.*

(who had transferred from Charleston), awaited the Union army at Bull Run-Manassas. McDowell attacked the Confederate left flank on Matthews Hill. The Union soldiers were momentarily able to dominate the battlefield but by late afternoon were forced to retreat when Confederate reinforcements arrived from the Shenandoah Valley. What had appeared to be a Union victory in the morning now turned into a rout as the Federal retreat deteriorated into a pell-mell rush to leave the battlefield. Spectators, who had come to the battlefield with their picnic baskets and who expected to see the quick dispersal of the Confederate army, joined the retreating Federal soldiers in their flight back to Washington.

For the fledgling Confederacy, the Battle of Bull Run-Manassas had been a dramatic and convincing success. Of the approximately 32,000 Southern troops involved in the battle, only 1,750 had been lost. Federal losses were estimated at 2,950. The door to Washington was open and all that was needed was for Confederate troops to complete their victory by occupying the Union capital. Although victorious, the Confederates were too disorganized to pursue the retreating Union forces off the battlefield. This inability to exploit the success at Bull Run-Manassas would haunt the Confederate States throughout its existence.

Just as Fort Sumter had diverted attention away from Pensacola, the Battle of Bull Run-Manassas clearly established Virginia as one of the major theaters of the war. Florida troops played no active role in this first major battle of the war, but Florida men were being hastily organized for service in Virginia. On July 13, just three days before this

*George Taliaferro Ward commanded the Second Florida Infantry Regiment when it was shipped to Virginia just after the Battle of Bull Run-Manassas. He was killed at the Battle of Williamsburg in 1862. (Drawing published in Francis P. Fleming,* A Memoir of C. Seton Fleming; *Francis P. Fleming Collection, Tebeau-Field Library of Florida History.)*

battle, the Second Florida Infantry Regiment, under the command Colonel George T. Ward of Leon County, was mustered into Confederate service near Jacksonville and sent immediately to Virginia. The initial term of enlistment was 12 months because Confederate authorities, like their Union counterparts, fully expected the war to be brief. Both sides would be terribly disappointed in their predictions.

With the failure of the Union army at Bull Run-Manassas, Federal authorities realized that an overall strategic plan for prosecuting a full-blown war was necessary. The result was the so-called "Anaconda Plan," a multi-faceted plan to strangle the Confederacy by splitting it along the Mississippi River and by capturing Richmond. In addition, the plan called for isolating the Confederacy from potential European supporters by imposing a naval blockade along the entire Southern coastline. The Confederates responded by creating defensive positions that would allow the maximum use of their limited resources. Although Florida troops participated in virtually all theaters of the war, large and small, their principal assignments were to the Army of Northern Virginia and the Army of Tennessee, which bore the brunt of fighting for the Confederacy.

Thus the major campaigns of what would be a four-year war were defined in the immediate aftermath of Bull Run-Manassas. The Federal government, chastened by defeat in its first offensive effort, quickly began to assemble and train new forces. In Washington, General McDowell was relieved of his command and replaced by Major General George B. McClellan, who set about reorganizing and training the Army of the Potomac. In the west, General John C. Fremont, the hero of the Republic of California,

*George B. McClellan assumed command of the Army of the Potomac following the disastrous Federal defeat at Bull Run-Manassas. (Library of Congress.)*

*The Second Florida Infantry Regiment was assigned to Major General John Bankhead Magruder's division during the Siege of Yorktown in 1862.*

commanded the Department of Missouri. A month after Bull Run-Manassas, he was replaced by Major General Henry W. Halleck, who was given responsibility for preventing Confederate control of the Mississippi. For some months, neither Confederate nor Federal forces in the western theater embarked on a major campaign, due primarily to the need of both sides to organize, train, and equip their forces.

The Second Florida reached Richmond on July 21, just five days after Bull Run-Manassas. For nearly two months the regiment was assigned to guard duty. On September 17, the regiment was moved to the vicinity of Yorktown on the Virginia peninsula. There they were assigned to the command of Major General John Bankhead Magruder. Yorktown, which had been the scene of Cornwallis's surrender in the American Revolution, was certain to be a major target of the Union army when campaigning resumed in the spring of 1862. To provide as much protection as possible against the anticipated Federal assault, Confederate troops erected substantial fortifications, and the Second Florida was part of this effort.

In the spring, General McClellan undertook the opening gambit in his campaign to capture Richmond by laying siege to Yorktown. Despite a Federal preponderance of men and materiel, the siege offered both armies an opportunity to test the effectiveness of the training they had received during the winter months. For McClellan, this kind of slow, methodical campaigning would become the hallmark of his career as a commander.

The siege of Yorktown marked the start of the Second Florida's outstanding record as a part of the Confederate campaigns in Virginia. In the opening stages of the siege, the unit, along with the Second Mississippi battalion, received a special notice from General Magruder when he wrote in one of his reports the following:

> The enemy's skirmishers pressed closely in front of Yorktown. Brigadier-General [Jubal] Early ordered a sortie to be made from the redoubts for the purpose of dislodging the enemy from Pulmentary's peach orchard. This was effected in the most brilliant manner by the Second Florida . . . . The quick and reckless charge of our men, by throwing the enemy into a hasty flight, enabled us to effect . . . an enterprise of great hazard, against a superior force supported by artillery, when the least wavering or hesitation on our part would have been attended with great loss.

On May 3, General Joseph E. Johnston, now in charge of the Confederate defenses on the peninsula, ordered a withdrawal from Yorktown to Williamsburg. McClellan sent his army in pursuit, and a fierce clash between the rear echelons of the retreating Confederates and the pursuing Federals precipitated a major battle. Johnston, a daring battlefield commander, rushed the main body of his army to the scene of the fighting. Additional Union troops were brought up until approximately 40,000 of them faced some 31,000 Confederates.

The battle at Williamsburg raged a full day as both armies sought control of fortifications that had been erected earlier in the year by General Magruder. During this battle, the Second Florida, although unattached to any specific unit, was placed into battle on the Confederate right flank. Here, along with the Second Mississippi, the Florida troops came under heavy assault. Despite their lack of extensive battle experience, the troops acquitted themselves well. The Second Florida paid a heavy price, however, including the death of its commander, Colonel George T. Ward. Casualty figures for the regiment were put at 37 killed, 152 wounded, and 9 missing.

After a full day's fighting, the numerically superior forces of McClellan were successful in securing a portion of the fortifications surrounding the city. Johnston, realizing that this allowed the Union army the opportunity to flank his own, ordered a general retreat from Williamsburg to the western side of the Chickahominy River in front of Richmond.

Although the siege at Yorktown and the battle of Williamsburg proved to be minor preludes to more desperate fighting, the sheer size of McClellan's army and those of other Federal armies operating in other areas of the state gave a sense of urgency to Richmond's calls for more troops for the Virginia campaigns. Although it had the smallest population of all the Confederate states, Florida responded by organizing the Fifth Infantry Regiment (April 8, 1862) and the Eighth Infantry Regiment (July 5, 1862). These two regiments joined the Second in the Army of Northern Virginia in time for the Confederate triumph at Second Bull Run-Manassas at the end of August 1862.

On May 31, General Johnston launched an attack against McClellan's army across the Chickahominy River at Fair Oaks-Seven Pines. The object was to force the Union army away from the Richmond defenses and back into the Virginia peninsula. Despite having a momentary advantage because McClellan had split his army and straddled the river, confusion among Confederate units negated this opportunity. Attacking in the early afternoon, the Confederate assault was soon bogged down. Johnston received a severe wound and was taken from the battlefield. General Gustavus W. Smith assumed temporary control of the Army of Northern Virginia for a few hours, but was replaced on June 1 by Robert E. Lee.

The outcome of the struggle at Fair Oaks-Seven Pines amounted to little more than a draw. Of the 42,000 Confederate soldiers, 6,100 were killed, missing, or wounded. For the 42,000 Union soldiers engaged in the battle, the number of casualties was estimated at 5,100. Since the Confederates were able to safely retreat to their fortifications and the Union army gained no appreciable advantage, Fair Oaks-Seven Pines technically was a stalemate. In reality, however, the Confederates could not afford to exchange casualties at a 1:1 or higher rate for very long, since the Union possessed a considerably larger reserve of manpower.

Throughout June and into July, the Second Florida, now assigned to Brigadier General Roger A. Pryor's Brigade in Longstreet's Division of the Army of Northern Virginia, participated in Lee's campaign to force McClellan from the gates of Richmond. From June 25 until July 1, the Confederate army, which had successfully consolidated its forces in Virginia and numbered approximately 90,000 men, drove the numerically superior (115,000) Federal army back to the James River. The Second Florida saw action at Beaver Dam Creek on June 26, Gaines' Mill on June 27, and at Frayser's Farm on June 30.

Lee's offensive campaign to push the Federal army away from the outskirts of Richmond was successful. Although the Federal forces enjoyed a considerable advantage in manpower and had several opportunities to turn the Confederate campaign into an overwhelming Union victory, McClellan's obsessive belief that Lee had been able to assemble an army of 200,000 led him to forsake these opportunities and retreat toward the James River. Despite the overall good showing of Federal troops and their successful retreat, Abraham Lincoln, who had already been at odds with McClellan's refusal to use his army with more vigor, removed him from command and replaced him with Major General John Pope.

The Seven Days campaign exacted a heavy toll on the victorious Confederates. Despite their overall success, the strenuous demands made in maneuvering the outnumbered Southern troops left them exhausted and weary. In addition, the campaign had levied a high toll of casualties. Overall, Southern casualties numbered 20,000, compared to the Federal total of 16,000. A Confederate victory on the field, perhaps, but a terrible defeat in lost manpower.

Following the Seven Days campaign, the newly formed Fifth Florida Infantry and the Eighth Florida Infantry Regiments joined the Second Florida in Pryor's Brigade. Along with the Twelfth Virginia and Fourteenth Alabama regiments, the Florida troops fought together for the first time in the battle of Second Bull Run-Manassas on August 28-30. Assigned to Longstreet's Division, these regiments were part of the largest massed infantry assault of the entire war on August 30, when some 28,000 Confederate troops crushed the left flank of a Union army under the command of Major General Pope. Brigade commander Pryor reported that in the battle "the Fifth and Eighth Florida regiments, though never under fire before, exhibited the cool and collected courage of veterans."

Following the success of Confederate arms at Second Bull Run-Manassas, Lee launched his famous Maryland Campaign, designed to carry the war to Union soil. After learning that Federal troops still occupied Harper's Ferry, Lee divided his army into four columns and sent three of them to eliminate this threat to the rear of the Confederate army. "Stonewall" Jackson, who had fought in the area many times, was placed in overall command of the Southern troops there.

Hard on the heels of their most recent battle, Florida troops were part of Jackson's capture of an entire Union army at Harper's Ferry. In three days of relatively minor fighting, some 12,419 Union soldiers surrendered. The cost in terms of Confederate casualties was only 39 killed and 247 wounded. Union casualties were equally light. Forty-four Federal soldiers were killed and 173 wounded. After the battle, Jackson left the Federal prisoners in the care of General A.P. Hill and hurried to join Lee in Maryland. (Hill paroled the prisoners, and he, too, hurried to join Lee.)

In the meantime, Lee had pressed on into Maryland. Facing him was the Federal Army of the Potomac, once again under the command of George B. McClellan. On September 14, his force encountered Lee's diminished army at South Mountain. In a series of hard-fought battles for the crucial mountain passes that controlled access to the area, the

*Major General Richard H. "Fighting Dick" Anderson, CSA.*

*Pictured here are Confederate dead killed at Bloody Lane, Antietam-Sharpsburg. (Library of Congress.)*

*Brigadier General Edward A.*
*Perry of the Second Florida*
*Infantry regiment.*

Federal army pushed the Confederates back and inflicted heavy casualties. Despite his apparent victory, McClellan delayed taking any follow-up action.

The Confederates took advantage of the Union failure to seize its victory at South Mountain by concentrating their forces at Sharpsburg on Antietam Creek. Jackson, who had moved swiftly after his victory at Harper's Ferry, arrived with his soldiers to reinforce Lee. The Florida regiments, temporarily assigned to the command of Major General R.H. "Fighting Dick" Anderson, were part of the reinforcements. On September 17, McClellan's army of 115,000 men faced Lee's force of 57,000 in what would become the single bloodiest day of combat in American military history. After a day filled with attacks and counterattacks, Union troops were poised to capture the entire Army of Northern Virginia. Only the timely arrival of A.P. Hill's division from Harper's Ferry prevented a complete rout of Lee's army. Although considerably outnumbered, the Confederates were able to fight the Union troops to a standstill. McClellan's timidity and the fear of committing all of his troops to battle allowed Lee to consolidate his positions. The toll had been extremely heavy, and some 23,000 Union and Confederate troops were killed or wounded.

Although both armies continued to skirmish the next day, McClellan failed to launch any concerted attack on Confederate lines. Indeed, the fighting was so disorganized and light that Lee began to move his wounded away from the battlefield and back into Virginia. Thus ended Lee's first invasion of the North.

*A lithograph of Fredericksburg, Virginia, 1863.*

Licking its wounds, the Army of Northern Virginia looked forward to taking up winter quarters to rest and recuperate for the next round of fighting in the spring. Florida troops had been in the forefront of the fighting at Antietam-Sharpsburg and had deported themselves well. Like other Southern units, the cost in men had been high, and when the army returned to Virginia, Lee began to reorganize it. All three Florida regiments were consolidated into a single brigade and placed under the command of Edward A. Perry, who had served as the colonel of the Second Florida and who was now promoted to brigadier general.

The Union Army of the Potomac was not quite ready to end its fighting season, however. Following his failure to gain a decisive victory at Antietam-Sharpsburg, McClellan was relieved of command for the second time. Major General Ambrose E. Burnside was placed in command and instructed by Abraham Lincoln to be aggressive in his actions. Burnside attempted to do just that, and on November 14, he sent a corps of the Union army to occupy Falmouth, near Fredericksburg.

Lee, anticipating that this was a prelude to the next major Union offensive, moved his army to the heights surrounding Fredericksburg and waited for Burnside to come. On November 11, Union engineers began laying five pontoon bridges across the Rappahannock River. Lee responded by ordering Confederate troops to halt the bridging effort. Two Mississippi regiments and the Eighth Florida regiment were assigned this task. For a full day, this small force managed to keep the Union army at bay. However, Federal artillery and musketry fire eventually drove the Confederates away. For the Eighth Florida, this opening gambit in the Battle of Fredericksburg resulted in the loss of 7 men killed, 24 wounded, and 20 captured. The remainder of the Florida brigade was not actively involved in the fighting.

On December 12, Burnside's army crossed the river and prepared to assault Confederate positions on the heights. The next day, December 13, the first Federal attacks were made. Wave after wave of Union troops were beaten back with horrific casualties. Despite a momentary breakthrough by Federal troops under the command of Major General George G. Meade, the Confederate lines were never seriously threatened. Despite continued Union efforts the next day, Lee's troops were simply too well entrenched and continued to rain devastating fire on the attacking troops. Burnside decided on December 15 that he would not be able to breach the Confederate lines in any significant way and began pulling his forces back across the Rappahannock. Fredericksburg was a disaster of epic proportions for the Union army. In three days of fighting, the United States lost approximately 13,400 killed or wounded soldiers, while the Confederacy's losses were placed at 4,600.

The Confederates looked forward to a period of extended rest and refitting during the winter, but Burnside, under tremendous pressure from Lincoln, undertook an abortive offensive in January 1863. The wet winter weather soon stalled the Union effort. Disappointed with Burnside's overall performance, Lincoln relieved him of command that same month and replaced him with Major General Joseph Hooker.

With only scattered fighting to occupy his attention, Lee began to plot his next offensive, but the Union army moved first. By April 30, 1864, General Hooker, feeling the same pressure from Washington as his predecessors had, decided to flank the Confederate army by crossing the Rappahannock and Rapidan Rivers north of Fredericksburg. Leaving a portion of his army to demonstrate before the Southern positions at Fredericksburg, Hooker hoped to take Lee by surprise. Divining Hooker's strategy, Lee left a covering force at Fredericksburg and moved to meet Hooker.

The Union advance encountered progressively stronger Confederate forces, and Hooker ordered a halt to his invasion. Concentrating his forces near Chancellorsville on May 1, he took up hastily constructed defensive positions. Lee, with a force of around 58,000, was ready to attack on May 2 and sent Stonewall Jackson's troops against the Union left. Jackson's initial attack was successful, but Federal troops rallied and stalled the Southern advance. That night, while making a reconnaissance of Union lines, Jackson was mortally wounded by his own troops. Jackson's death, according to many scholars, was the single greatest loss the Southern army experienced in the war.

The Florida brigade had been part of the Confederate covering force at Fredericksburg, but were ordered out of their positions on the night of May 2 and marched to join Lee's army at Chancellorsville. On the morning of May 3, the brigade took part in the heaviest fighting, which occurred in the so-called "Furnace." Their bravery and execution of orders, particularly that of the Fifth and Second Florida, earned them a special notice in the battle report filed afterwards by General R.H. Anderson. He noted that their conduct "through the tiresome marching and continued watching, as well as while engaging the enemy, was such as to merit high praise."

*Thomas J. "Stonewall" Jackson, CSA.*

Chancellorsville was an overwhelming Confederate victory and, despite the loss of Jackson, is considered by many historians to be Lee's finest victory. Hooker had committed some 97,000 Union troops to the battle, easily outnumbering Lee's forces by some 40,000, but suffered some 4,000 more battle casualties. Forced to leave the field to Lee, Hooker could take little solace in the news that Federal Major General John Sedgwick had managed to drive the remaining Confederate forces off the heights at Fredericksburg. When Sedgwick attempted to move his force to join Hooker in his new positions, he ran into Lee and the Army of Northern Virginia and was soundly defeated. By May 6, Hooker realized that nothing could salvage his defeat at Lee's hands, and he ordered his army to the north bank of the Rappahannock.

The Florida brigade had suffered 20 killed and 86 wounded. While every soldier was irreplaceable, the Florida brigade's casualties were not particularly heavy at Chancellorsville. That, however, would change in the next campaign.

In early June, Lee decided to carry the war to the Union. By using the Shenandoah Valley as a screen for his movements, he hoped to strike a decisive blow to Union war efforts by creating fear and apprehension among the civilian population. In part, Lee's invasion was a psychological counterbalance to Lincoln's Emancipation Proclamation, which became final in January. Although accomplishing little in real terms, the Proclamation was favorably received by Europeans, who brought pressure on their governments to deny formal recognition to the Confederates States. A successful invasion of the Northern heartland would negate much of the Proclamation's impact.

With J.E.B. Stuart's cavalry in the lead, the Army of Northern Virginia headed north. For almost three weeks, the army met only token resistance by Federal troops. The Army of the Potomac, still commanded by Hooker, seemed paralyzed as Lee's forces moved out of the Shenandoah Valley into Maryland. On June 27, Hooker asked Lincoln to be relieved of command. Lincoln, frustrated by Hooker's inaction and embarrassed by Lee's invasion, immediately placed George G. Meade at the head of the army. Meade, informed that Lee's army was at Chambersburg and was headed for Gettysburg, ordered three full corps to intercept them there. By July 1, Meade managed to get about 84,000 troops to Gettysburg.

Lee's troops, numbering some 75,000, attacked the Union positions from the north and west. The initial Confederate assault pushed the Federal troops out of Gettysburg to the outlying Cemetery Hill, and thus ended the first day of battle. Although both sides received reinforcements that night, the Union army maintained its numerical superiority. On July 2, Lee continued his attack and attempted to drive the Federals off the hills.

*This monument is dedicated to Florida soldiers who fought and died at Gettysburg. (Photograph by Virginia J. Taylor.)*

LEFT: *Francis P. Fleming was one of the Florida soldiers who fought in all the major battles in Virginia. He later became governor of Florida. (Fleming Collection, Tebeau-Field Library of Florida History.)* RIGHT: *David Lang was the commander of the Florida Brigade at Gettysburg. (Valentine Museum, Richmond.)*

Although they were somewhat successful, the Confederates could not carry the Union positions. When darkness fell and the fighting stopped, Meade's men held their lines along Little Round Top.

Lee's men had managed to gain a tenuous position on Culp's Hill. On the morning of July 3, a determined effort by the Union soldiers drove the Confederates off the hill. After a mid-morning pause, Lee resumed the attack with an artillery bombardment and an infantry attack on the Union center located on Cemetery Ridge. Despite a determined Confederate charge, led by Major General George E. Pickett, which momentarily penetrated the Union line, the Southern effort was beaten back with severe casualties.

On July 4, Lee began his retreat from Gettysburg, through Maryland, to Virginia. It was reported that the wagon train carrying wounded Confederate soldiers stretched some 17 miles. The number of Southern dead was between 2,500 and 4,500, while the wounded numbered approximately 13,000 and another 5,000 were reported as missing. Although Union casualties were slightly higher, Gettysburg was an undeniable Confederate loss. Lee had lost fully one-third of his army—losses that could not be replaced.

The Florida brigade had been in the thick of the fighting throughout the battle. On July 2, the brigade had been part of a general charge of Federal artillery by General James

Longstreet. Despite a successful assault that resulted in the capture of the Union guns, the brigade was forced to retreat soon afterward. During this charge, the Eighth Florida lost its regimental colors when the color bearer was killed. On July 3, the brigade was placed in support of the Confederate artillery that prefaced Pickett's charge up Cemetery Ridge. When that charge failed, the Florida brigade and Brigadier General Cadmus M. Wilcox's brigade was sent in 20 minutes later on a second attempt to take the ridge. During this unsuccessful charge, the Second Florida "lost their colors and a greater part of their men."

Gettysburg ended the effectiveness of the Florida brigade as a separate fighting force. Although it continued to be called a brigade and to fight in other battles, it now numbered less than had a full regiment in 1861. Colonel David Lang, who had commanded the brigade at Gettysburg, reported to General Perry on July 19 that the unit had been reduced to a mere 22 officers and 233 enlisted men. He listed the total casualties at Gettysburg as 33 killed, 211 wounded, and 211 missing.

The Florida brigade was not the only unit to suffer such high casualties. Never again would the Army of Northern Virginia conduct an offensive campaign. Although badly wounded, it did possess enough of a sting to be a force to be reckoned with, and the army could still embarrass an unwary Union commander. Meade would discover this as he pursued Lee's retreating army.

As Lee retreated toward Virginia, Meade sought to follow up the success of the Union army at Gettysburg. Delayed by his numerous wounded and the rain-swollen Potomac

*Floridians served valiantly in the frontlines of the battle at Missionary Ridge in Chattanooga. (Library of Congress.)*

River, Lee ordered the Army of Northern Virginia to construct defensive positions to protect the river crossings at Williamsport. While they waited for the river to go down, Meade attacked the Confederates with overwhelming force on July 13. Lee was able to hold his positions while his engineers constructed a bridge over the rapidly falling river. As night fell, he ordered his army across the river, leaving a small force to guard the rear. Although Meade was able to rout this rearguard force and take some 500 prisoners, he was not able to do further damage to Lee's main force. The Army of Northern Virginia was back on its home soil.

Events in Virginia took a backseat to Bragg's developing campaign against Chattanooga. In early September, Lee sent two full divisions to assist the Army of Tennessee in its attempts to crush the Union invasion of Georgia. Realizing the importance of this confrontation, Meade dispatched two corps to bolster the Union defense of this strategic objective. Immediately following the Battle of Chickamauga (September 18–20), Lee sought to exploit Meade's weakened army by sending his remaining troops around Federal positions along the Rapidan River. Thus began the Bristoe Campaign, a series of inconclusive conflicts that ended with a Union victory at Rappahannock Station on November 7. The end result of more than a month of maneuvering and skirmishing was the further loss of much needed fighting men by Lee. The Army of Northern Virginia lost approximately 5,000 troops overall, including the capture of 1,600 soldiers at Rappahannock Station.

Looking for time to rest and replenish his army, Lee disengaged his forces after this battle and moved to winter quarters south of the Rapidan River. Almost immediately, Meade tried to take advantage of the tired and ravaged Army of Northern Virginia. In late November, he sent his army through the Wilderness to attack the Confederate forces at Payne's farm and New Hope Church. Although Meade had some 25,000 more troops than did Lee, he was not able to break through the Confederate lines on November 30, the first full day of battle. When Lee moved his troops into a series of prepared field positions during the night, Meade made only a half-hearted effort the next day to breach them. He withdrew his forces on December 2. And so ended the campaigns of 1863.

The year had been a costly one for Confederate forces in Virginia. Despite early victories in the spring, the Gettysburg campaign had levied a heavy toll in terms of casualties. Many of the units in the Army of Northern Virginia were operating at one-third to one-half strength. As winter set in, Confederate authorities issued a desperate call to the states for more troops.

In April, Colonel John M. Morgan organized the Florida Ninth Infantry Regiment, a consolidated unit made up of the Sixth Florida Infantry Battalion and three independent companies. It was immediately shipped to Lee in Virginia and participated in the opening campaigns of 1864. In early June, the Florida Tenth Infantry Regiment, created by the consolidation of First Special Infantry Battalion and four companies of the Second Infantry Battalion, was brought on line. It, too, was rushed to Virginia and immediately entered the trenches surrounding Petersburg. The last Florida unit to be created was the Florida Eleventh Infantry Regiment, created by merging the Fourth Infantry Battalion with two companies of the Second Infantry Battalion and one independent company. Commanded by Colonel Theodore W. Brevard, it entered Confederate service at

*General Ulysses
Simpson Grant,
USA. (Library of
Congress.)*

Petersburg within days of its creation. These regiments represented the bottom of the manpower reserves in Florida. When they were killed or captured, there would be no more forthcoming.

The spring campaign of 1864 was very different than those of the previous three years. Abraham Lincoln, frustrated by the failure of so many of his commanders to use the numerical superiority of the Union army to relentlessly pursue and destroy the Confederate army, appointed Ulysses S. Grant as the commander of all Federal armies. Grant, who had emerged as the best Union commander in the western theater, was now given the job of finishing off Lee. Sometimes criticized as having very little tactical brilliance, he nevertheless was willing to fight a war of attrition against Lee. Fully aware that any losses he sustained could be immediately replaced by fresh troops, Grant was also aware that each casualty suffered by the Army of Northern Virginia meant a permanent reduction in available manpower. Thus emerged the Union strategy for the remainder of the war—strike constantly, trade casualty for casualty, and, most importantly, avoid any major mistakes that would allow Lee to gain the upper hand. Draws and defeats in battle were acceptable to Grant, but retreat was out of the question.

The Wilderness campaign of May 5–7, with the capture of Richmond as its objective, launched the beginning of this new strategy. Fielding an army of more than 100,000, Grant

LEFT: *A pre-war resident of Fernandina, General Joseph J. Finegan was the Confederate general who won the Battle of Olustee in north Florida. He also commanded the Florida Brigade in Lee's army. (Florida State Archives.)*
RIGHT: *Here is a 14-year-old Confederate soldier killed in Petersburg in 1865. (Library of Congress.)*

attacked Lee's army of approximately 61,000. Although two days of fierce fighting resulted in the loss of 18,500 Federal casualties to only 11,500 for the Confederates, Lee was forced to retreat when Grant disengaged his soldiers and sent them around the left flank toward Richmond. The Florida brigade, who had been in the thick of the fighting, was decimated by the loss of approximately 250 men.

Lee was forced by this maneuver to retreat, and a day later, the two armies met again at Spotsylvania Courthouse. For almost two weeks, Grant's army, which had been reinforced to bring its strength back to around 100,000 men, struggled to defeat Lee's. Despite some success, such as the attack against the "Bloody Angle," which resulted in the capture of an entire Confederate division, Grant had to settle for another inconclusive result on the field. The war of attrition had been won entirely by Grant, however, whose army had lost 18,000 men, but had inflicted some 12,000 casualties on Lee's Confederates.

Grant disengaged his forces on May 21 and began a flanking movement toward Richmond. Lee hastily withdrew to interpose his army between Grant and the capital. Both armies received reinforcements in anticipation of another round of fighting. Grant now had 108,000 soldiers at his disposal, a dramatic increase in the size of the Federal force. Even Lee had managed to add some 20,000 new soldiers, bringing his total to 62,000. Among these new troops was the Florida Ninth Regiment.

New fighting erupted ten days later at Cold Harbor when Federal troops confronted the Confederates entrenched in fortifications that stretched some seven miles. For almost two weeks the two armies pounded each other. Although Lee won a resounding victory, exchanging a total of 13,000 Federal casualties for only 2,500 of his own, he did not crush Grant. On June 12, Grant moved his army out of Cold Harbor and headed south toward Petersburg.

The Florida Brigade, now reinforced by the Florida Ninth, Tenth, and Eleventh regiments and under the command of General Joseph J. Finegan, had been in the thick of the action at Cold Harbor. The consolidated brigade, now referred to as Finegan's Brigade, numbered about 600 men. During the battle, the unit suffered heavy casualties. The newly arrived Florida Ninth lost 100 men killed or wounded. The Second, Fifth, and Eighth Regiments, in action since 1862, had a combined strength of only 200 effectives. Many of these were killed or captured during the battle. Once lost, these men were never replaced, and the brigade continued to shrink.

Federal and Confederate units had clashed at Petersburg on June 9. A Confederate force of about 2,500 soldiers, under the command of General P.G.T. Beauregard, had beaten off a probing attack by some 4,500 Federal troops. Because the bulk of Confederate soldiers were "old men and young boys" assigned to the Virginia Home Guard, this small conflict is frequently referred to by that name.

Once again, Lee was forced to move his army to meet the persistent threat of Grant's maneuvering. Moving rapidly to arrive at Petersburg before the Federal army could take the city, the Army of Northern Virginia slid into prepared fortifications in front just in time. Finegan's Florida Brigade was placed in the front trenches of the Confederate position after a forced march of some 50 miles. For three days, they were exposed to intense artillery fire as Grant tried to break through the lines before Lee could strengthen his siege defenses.

*Union troops take a break from the fighting at Petersburg. (U.S. Military History Institute.)*

Petersburg became the locus of the war in Virginia for the next ten months. Desperate to hold Petersburg and protect Richmond, Lee concentrated his forces and dug in. With Sherman marching steadily toward Atlanta and Grant firmly lodged before Petersburg, the long war had reached its decisive final stage.

Finegan's Brigade continued to be used in most of the skirmishes in and around Petersburg. On June 23, the brigade was sent to drive away a Union force destroying sections of the Weldon railroad. On June 30, the brigade marched 10 miles to confront an enemy force at Ream's Station, which was driven back. On August 21, the brigade was part of a Confederate attack on entrenched Union positions on the Weldon railroad. Here the brigade experienced a "loss in killed and wounded [that] was very severe." In early December, the brigade participated in a strike against a Federal raiding party near Bellfield. After a march of some 50 miles, General A.P. Hill's Third Corps forced a Union army of 20,000 to retreat.

The march to Bellfield brought the year to a close. For all but the most optimistic Confederate, the signs were clearly evident—the hope for an independent Southern nation had been lost on the open fields of Gettysburg. The best that could be hoped for was a stalemate, but even that looked impossible. In Georgia, Sherman's army had taken Savannah in late December and there were only the remnants of the Army of Tennessee

*Brigadier General Theodore W. Brevard led the Florida Brigade during the last days of the Civil War. (Florida State Archives.)*

left to block his path to Virginia. Balancing Sherman's threat to Lee's army was the possibility that the Army of Tennessee might be able to join Lee's Army of Northern Virginia and extend the war. When Joseph E. Johnston was again placed in command of this ragtag army, the union of the two Southern forces looked more and more possible.

The Confederates remained in the trenches at Petersburg during January, February, and early March. Grant's forces continued their probing actions against the Southern defenses on a regular basis. Units of the Federal army attempted different flanking maneuvers in an effort to cut off Lee's reinforcements and supplies. Lincoln was still calling for an all-out push against Lee and the conclusion of the war by early summer.

On February 5, 6, and 7, Finegan's Brigade was moved out of the shelter of the defensive lines at Petersburg and sent to assist Major General John B. Gordon, who was facing a Union force of some 35,000 troops at Hatcher's Run. In three days of desperate fighting, Gordon, who had only 14,000 Confederate troops, managed to halt the Union advance. The Federal lines, however, were extended to that point. After this battle at Hatcher's Run, Finegan's Brigade returned to their positions.

On March 25, Lee tried a desperate and futile offensive against Grant's army. Placing one-half of his meager forces under the command of Gordon, Lee directed him to break through the Union lines and threaten the Federal supply depot at City Point. Although

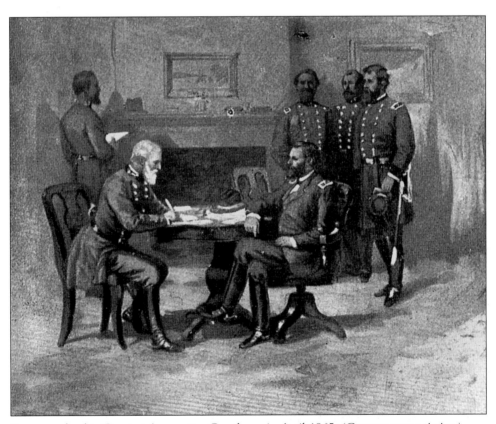

*Lee surrendered to Grant at Appomattox Courthouse in April 1865. (Contemporary painting.)*

Gordon was able to overpower the garrisons of Fort Stedman, the Union counterattack pushed him back. More than 1,900 Confederate soldiers were captured, and the Union army captured the Confederate entrenchments in front of them. Grant now had a key to the lock of Confederate defenses at Petersburg, and the path to Richmond beckoned invitingly.

Marshalling his forces, Grant quickly exploited the weak spot, and on April 2, his army broke through Lee's lines in force. Unable to stem the flood of Union soldiers, Lee ordered his men to abandon their positions and retreat toward Appomattox Courthouse. Richmond was lost, and the Confederate government was forced to flee for their lives.

The Florida Brigade, now under the command of Brigadier Theodore W. Brevard, was part of the Confederate rearguard that attempted to delay Grant's army. Near Farmville, on April 6, Brevard led the Fifth, Eighth, and Eleventh Florida Regiments in a skirmish against cavalry troops of Brigadier General George Armstrong Custer. Tired, exhausted, and outnumbered, the small force was captured. The remainder of the brigade continued on toward Appomattox Courthouse, where Lee, on April 9, ordered one last attack in an effort to break though the ring of Federal forces surrounding his army. Although initially successful in his early morning attack, he was soon stopped by the arrival of Union infantry in force. Faced with the realization that the final defeat of the Army of Northern Virginia was at hand, Lee sent an emissary to Grant asking for terms of surrender.

Although Johnston still controlled a small army in North Carolina and although the Confederacy still had a significant number of troops west of the Mississippi River, the reality was that after four long and bloody years the war was over. Those, too, would be surrendered during the following month.

For the survivors of the Florida Brigade, Appomattox meant that they were now free to return to their homes to try to make sense of a world turned upside down.

# 4. On Distant Fields
## The Western Theater

As Southern state after Southern state withdrew from the Union, Federal authorities were reluctant to force a direct confrontation between the U.S. Army and the state troops that seized the small arsenals and interior forts of the region. In general, the small detachments of Federal troops that served in these outposts surrendered them without hesitation to state militias, and only a few attempts were made to disable the arms and ammunition stored there. Indeed, some Federal commanders were sympathetic to the cause of Southern independence and ensured that their subordinates did nothing to damage the arms and ammunition stored there.

Across the region, small units of U.S. troops were concentrated in coastal forts that could be reinforced or supplied by Federal ships without the necessity of putting troops ashore on the mainland. In Key West, long a major naval center, Federal military authorities strengthened Fort Taylor in preparation for a surprise attack by Florida troops. Their apprehension, in reality, was unwarranted and they had little to fear because of the isolated nature of the Florida Keys. Out in the Gulf of Mexico, Fort Jefferson, only recently completed, was reinforced with additional troops and arms. The very nature of this fortification, alone and accessible only by ship, ensured that no serious attempt would be made against it in 1861 or in subsequent years.

The eyes of the entire American population, both North and South, focused instead on Fort Sumter in Charleston and Fort Pickens in Pensacola where Federal troops defied local and state authorities. Strategically located in such a way as to deny effective use of these major harbors, Fort Sumter and Fort Pickens were graphic reminders that Southern independence would never be a reality as long as Federal forces held these bastions. In South Carolina, Southern troops erected batteries along the shore to confront Sumter's guns. For several months, both sides were content to watch each other warily through the sights of their cannons.

Following Florida's declaration of independence in early January, a similar scene was played out in Pensacola. There, Colonel William H. Chase, the individual, who, as a Federal officer, had supervised the construction of Fort Pickens, commanded some 1,700 state troops from Alabama and Florida arrayed on the shoreline against the fortress. Tensions were extremely high and fraught with peril. On January 12, just two days after the passage of the Secession Ordinance by the Florida Convention, a delegation of three Southern officers made their way to the fort to demand its surrender. Lieutenant Adam Slemmer, the Federal officer in charge of the fort, summarily rejected this demand. On January 15, Chase, along with Captain Ebenezer Farrand, former deputy commander of the Pensacola Navy Yard, crossed the small channel that separated Pickens from the city and demanded the surrender of the fort. This second demand, as well as a third demand made a few days later, was also rejected. It appeared that nothing could stop the rapid escalation into war.

Disturbed by the overwhelming preponderance of Confederate troops deployed by Southern forces in Pensacola, Federal officials in Washington prepared to reinforce Pickens, just as it had done at Forts Taylor and Jefferson.

There were those, North and South, who still hoped for either reconciliation or a peaceful compromise that would allow Southern states to secede peacefully. These men urged both sides to exercise caution, lest either side force the other into a violent confrontation from which neither side could withdraw. In Washington, prominent Southern politicians, some of whom had officially withdrawn from their positions in the Federal government, used their influence and established contacts to bring about an unofficial and uneasy peace agreement that prevented immediate fighting. The United

*Major Robert Anderson refused to surrender Fort Sumter in Charleston Harbor without a fight. (Leslie's Illustrated Newspaper.)*

*This is a view of Fort Pickens in Pensacola Harbor.* (Leslie's Illustrated Newspaper.)

States could continue to occupy these forts without fear of Southern attack as long as no attempt was made to reinforce them. With this tacit understanding in place, all parties anxiously awaited the inauguration of Abraham Lincoln and wondered what the new president would do.

Although there was a military standoff in Southern states, activity on the political front proceeded at a rapid pace. Delegations from the seceded states met in Montgomery, Alabama, to create a new Southern national government. In March 1861, these delegates created the provisional Confederate States of America and immediately began to implement measures that would bring this paper agreement into reality. Jefferson Davis, a well-known Mississippian with experience as a military officer, a member of both houses of Congress, and a former secretary of war, was elected president. Davis, warily watching the unfolding of events in Washington, hastily appointed a cabinet and created a national army. Member states were asked to provide a 11,700 troops for the new national army. Florida's assessment was for 500 soldiers.

In Pensacola, command of the Florida and Alabama troops facing Fort Pickens was handed over to Braxton E. Bragg, a West Pointer with experience in the Mexican-American War and a longtime Mississippi acquaintance of Davis. In South Carolina, Pierre Gustave Toutant Beauregard, another West Point graduate from Louisiana, now in Confederate service, took command of the Confederate troops opposing Fort Sumter. Throughout the region, troops in each state prepared to change their status from state militia to Confederate soldiers as the Southern effort to assert its sovereignty gathered momentum.

*Braxton E. Bragg was a Mississippi planter and intimate of Jefferson Davis. As a general, he was roundly despised by the troops of the Army of Tennessee. Joseph E. Johnston replaced him after his defeat at Chattanooga. Bragg served as Davis's military advisor for the remainder of the war. (Library of Congress.)*

In Florida, Governor Madison Starke Perry, soon to be replaced by arch-secessionist John Milton, ordered state troops to the Chattahoochee Arsenal on April 5 for the purpose of fulfilling the request for national troops. Companies from Leon, Alachua, Franklin, Jackson, Madison, Gadsden, Jefferson, and Escambia Counties, all counties dominated by the state's planter elites, converged on the appointed site. These units were consolidated into the Florida First Infantry Regiment, under the command of prominent Jefferson County resident James Patton Anderson. Following its organization, the Florida First was ordered to Pensacola, and, on April 12, the regiment reported to Bragg's headquarters for duty assignments. The regiment remained in the Pensacola area for about a year but, with the exception of the small battle on Santa Rosa Island in the fall of 1861, saw very little action.

In the meantime, events were accelerating in other areas of the South. In Charleston Harbor, Major Robert Anderson refused the surrender demands by Confederates. On April 12, General Beauregard ordered Confederate batteries in Charleston to commence firing on Fort Sumter. Federal forces in the fort could offer only a token resistance to the shelling, and by early afternoon of the next day, Anderson was ready to surrender. War was now a reality.

The events in Charleston immediately took the pressure off Confederate troops around Pensacola. The conflict there touched off another round of state secession, and Virginia, North Carolina, Tennessee, and Arkansas severed their ties with the Union within the month immediately following the attack on Sumter. For the South, this meant a change in military strategy and a re-thinking of the best ways to protect the new nation. With

Virginia's decision to secede came a decision to re-locate the capital of the Confederacy from Montgomery to Richmond, barely 100 miles from the Union capital of Washington, D.C. The Confederacy was no longer a small band of Deep South states that could be dealt with on a piecemeal basis.

Following their victory at Bull Run-Manassas, Confederate authorities hastily appealed to the various states for additional troops. In Florida, the shift of emphasis away from Fort Pickens and Pensacola produced a stalemate that was only occasionally broken by exchanges of cannon fire and the small skirmish on Santa Rosa Island. When the Federal government began its buildup along the Ohio River, Southern authorities ordered the movement of troops concentrated around Pensacola and Mobile, Alabama, northward to join the command of General Albert S. Johnston in Mississippi. The Florida First, having completed its initial enlistment in the spring of 1862, was reorganized as the First Florida Infantry Regiment and sent north to serve with the division commanded by Brigadier General Daniel Ruggles. Colonel James Patton Anderson, who had commanded the regiment since its creation, was promoted to brigadier general and given command of a brigade.

In April 1862, the Florida First was dispatched to Corinth, Mississippi, where General Johnston was intent on attacking the Federal Army of the Tennessee, under the command of Major General Ulysses S. Grant. Johnston's decision to attack came after Union troops had been successful in capturing Forts Henry and Donelson on the Tennessee and Cumberland Rivers. Confederate plans for occupying and fortifying Kentucky along the Ohio River were frustrated. Fearful that Grant would be unstoppable in moving south

*Confederate soldiers in the field await orders to march. (Pace Library, University of West Florida.)*

*The first major battle experience for Florida troops in the Army of Tennessee came at the Battle of Shiloh. (Contemporary print.)*

along the Mississippi River if he was allowed to join his army with the Army of the Ohio, commanded by General Don Carlos Buell, Johnston moved his army north toward Grant's army at Shiloh.

Unaware of the Confederate movement, Grant and his subordinates allowed their troops to relax with a day of drilling and rest. Meanwhile, Johnston had managed to move his entire force to within striking distance of Grant's army without being detected. Despite a minor skirmish with a few outlying Union pickets the night before, Johnston managed to catch the Federal forces completely by surprise when he launched his attack on the morning of April 6. In rapid succession, Confederate soldiers overran each Union position. Only the dogged six-hour stand by Brigadier Benjamin M. Prentiss, commander of the Union Sixth Division, at the sunken road known as the "Hornet's Nest," allowed other Federal troops the opportunity to withdraw. Grant's army was saved by the arrival of Buell's troops during the night.

The next morning, tired Confederate units were pushed back over the same ground they had paid a bloody price to capture the day before. Unable to stem the tide of Buell's fresh units, General P.G.T. Beauregard, Johnston's second-in-command, ordered the Southern army to retreat south toward Corinth. Licking their wounds and feeling the loss of some 13,000 killed or missing troops, Union generals allowed the Confederates to disengage and move off the battlefield.

Although most of the soldiers of both armies were inexperienced, they fought with great tenacity. For the Confederates, the battle, although technically a victory in terms of casualties, had been a costly defeat in reality. General Johnston, an aggressive and capable commander, was wounded and bled to death on the battlefield. Some 10,500 Southern soldiers lost their lives. Individual units suffered horrific casualties and the Florida First was no exception. Its old commander, James P. Anderson, noted in his battle report that the unit had fought bravely and, despite severe casualties, had brought "new luster to the arms of the State they represented, and paints imperishable fame upon the colors they so proudly bore."

On May 2, the Florida First, which had been merged with the Confederate Guards response battalion from Louisiana, was part of the skirmish at Farmington, outside Corinth. This minor battle, a prelude to Union General Halleck's siege of Corinth, was costly for the Confederates, who counted 30 soldiers killed, while Federal forces lost only 2. Withdrawing into Corinth, the unit participated in the brief siege of the city until Beauregard ordered a Confederate withdrawal to Tupelo.

On July 17, 1862, the Florida First was separated from the Confederate Guards and, less than a month later, was consolidated with Lieutenant Colonel William Miller's Third Infantry Battalion on August 15. The combined unit took the name, the Florida First Reorganized Infantry Regiment. On April 9, 1865, the First Reorganized Infantry Regiment was consolidated with the Florida First Cavalry, the Third, Fourth, Sixth, and Seventh Infantry Regiments to emerge as the Florida First Consolidated Infantry Regiment, a designation it kept until April 26, 1865, when it surrendered at Durham Station, North Carolina.

Just as was the case with units from other Confederate states, Florida units were periodically reorganized or consolidated as the Southern manpower pool continued to

*Unites States vice-president John C. Breckinridge (of the Buchanan Administration) commanded some Florida troops at the Battle of Lebanon Pike in Tennessee in December 1862. (National Archives.)*

shrink with each passing battle and every campaign. Once assigned to a Confederate army in a particular theater, units tended to remain there until the end of the war. As a result, it is rather difficult to trace the activities of a single unit throughout the war. Complicating the picture even further is the now quaint habit of referring to units by the last name of their commanders. When a particular commander was killed or replaced, the unit's name also changed. Thus a single unit might be referred to by several different designations.

On July 25, 1861, Colonel William S. Dilworth organized the Florida Third Infantry Regiment. The regiment was mustered into Confederate service on August 11 of that year for an initial 12-month enlistment. Assigned to duty in Florida during its first year of existence, the Third Regiment participated in the Battle of Smyrna (Florida) on March 23, 1862, and the Battle of Brick Church the next day. On May 10, 1862, the regiment was reorganized and enlistments extended for the duration of the war. In June 1862, the Third Regiment received orders to join Braxton E. Bragg's army in Mississippi. When the regiment got to Montgomery, Alabama, its orders were changed and the unit was assigned to temporary duty in Mobile. In August, new orders were issued and the Third was transferred to Chattanooga, Tennessee.

At Chattanooga, the regiment was assigned to General John C. Brown's Brigade in James Patton Anderson's Division. The Florida First was also a part of this brigade, and both units participated in Bragg's invasion of Kentucky during late September and early

October. On October 8, 1862, Brown's Brigade was in the thick of the fighting at Perryville and both regiments were decimated. When Bragg was forced to retreat from Kentucky back into Tennessee, the two were little more than regiments in name only.

Following Bragg's disastrous Tennessee invasion, the First and Third Regiments were consolidated in December 1862 to form the Florida Regiment. In June 1861, the Florida Fourth Regiment was organized and mustered into Confederate service. Although assigned to various duty stations in Florida for its first year of existence, the Fourth was reorganized in May 1862 and ordered out of Florida to Corinth, Mississippi. Like the Third Regiment, the Fourth was temporarily assigned to Mobile. In October, however, the unit received orders to join Palmer's Brigade in the Army of Tennessee. On December 28, the Fourth, along with the First and Third, were brigaded to General William Preston in General John C. Breckinridge's command and saw heavy action for the first time in the skirmish at Lebanon Pike.

From December 31 until January 3, 1863, the Fourth was part of the major battle at Murfreesboro. Although the Florida units deported themselves well in this decisive battle, they suffered horrific casualties. The First and Third Regiments, which had a combined total of 531 men, lost 138 killed, wounded, or missing. This amounted to slightly more than 25 percent of their total strength. The Fourth, which entered the battle with 458 soldiers, lost a total of 194, or 42 percent of its effective strength.

Despite what appeared to be an early Confederate victory, Bragg decided that the Federal army under General William S. Rosecrans was ultimately going to prevail and ordered the withdrawal of Southern troops south to Tullahoma. Bragg's decision to withdraw capped a week of disheartening losses for the Confederacy. Along the Mississippi River, Federal General William T. Sherman pounded the approaches to the Vicksburg fortifications where Confederate forces held control of the river. In Washington in 1862, President Abraham Lincoln successfully changed the very nature of the war when he issued the Emancipation Proclamation. No longer were North and South fighting a military conflict—Lincoln had transformed Northern participation into a moral crusade against slavery. Potential European support for the fledgling Confederacy began to slowly wane.

Following the engagement at Murfreesboro, the Confederates went into winter camp. Given time to reorganize and recuperate, the Florida brigade was soon ready for additional duties. In May 1863, it was combined with the 47th Georgia Regiment and placed under the command of Brigadier General M.A. Stovall. Stovall's brigade was part of a larger force under the command of General Joseph Eggleston Johnston, who had been assigned overall responsibility for Confederate armies in Tennessee and Mississippi, which hoped to relieve the Federal siege of Vicksburg. Moving slowly westward, the Confederate force reached the Black River outside the beleaguered city on July 5, one day after Lieutenant General John C. Pemberton had surrendered the city.

Johnston retreated back to Jackson, with Federal forces in hot pursuit. In a short-lived siege of Jackson, Florida troops comported themselves in a notable fashion. On July 12, Johnston noted that "a party of skirmishers of the First, Third and Fourth Florida, Forty-seventh Georgia and Cobb's battery, struck the enemy's flank and captured 200 prisoners, and [the] colors of the Twenty-seventh, Forty-first, and Fifty-third Illinois regiments."

*Major General William S. Rosecrans, USA.*

While the Stovall's Brigade was engaged in Mississippi, Bragg's Army of Tennessee faced a new offensive by Rosecrans's Federal force. Rosecrans, determined to further split the Confederacy and to gain control of the important railroad crossroads at Chattanooga, decided to drive Bragg from his defensive lines around Tullahoma. On June 22, he launched a major offensive along several points. For the next seven days, Confederate troops were forced back by Union attacks. Particularly devastating for the Confederates were those engagements fought with Federal soldiers armed with the new Spencer seven-shot repeater rifles, which provided an already numerically superior army with the ability to throw up an unmatched hail of fire. Faced with a campaign that was spread over many miles, Bragg decided to withdraw from Tullahoma and to fall back on Chattanooga. On July 3, Federal troops under Major General Philip Sheridan occupied the abandoned Confederate positions.

Although the Confederates acquitted themselves well at Jackson, it was inevitable that the larger Federal forces would eventually overwhelm their defenses. As a result, Johnston abandoned his positions and the Southern army retreated eastward. On August 26, 1863, the Florida units were ordered to rejoin Bragg's army at Chattanooga. Before they could make their way to that city, Bragg was forced to retreat southward to LaFayette, Georgia, where the units rejoined the Army of Tennessee. After a brief rest, they were ordered to cross the Chickamauga River on September 18 and to take up positions on the right flank of the Confederate army.

Two additional Florida infantry regiments, the Sixth and Seventh, were also ordered into the lines at Chickamauga. The Sixth, organized in April 1862 and mustered into the Confederate army at that time, had been assigned various duties with the Department of East Tennessee until mid-1863 when it was ordered to join the Army of Tennessee at Tullahoma. From there the Sixth Florida was part of the army's efforts to stem the onslaught of the Federal forces moving south.

The Seventh Florida was also mustered into Confederate service in April 1862. Like the Sixth, the Seventh had been assigned to the Department of East Tennessee and participated in a number of small skirmishes. After a brief assignment to guard salt works in West Virginia, the Seventh was ordered back to Tennessee. In September 1863, the Seventh Florida, along with the Sixth, was assigned to Bate's Division of the Army of Tennessee, just in time for the Battle of Chickamauga.

Having lost Chattanooga when Rosecrans sent Federal troops across the Tennessee River in early September, Bragg was determined to regain this important rail link. The first skirmishes of this important battle began shortly after dawn on the morning of September 19. Union and Confederate infantry units clashed at Jay's Mill, and the battle spread from that point. Despite desperate and often hand-to-hand combat throughout the day, the Union forces held firm. The next day, however, Rosecrans made a critical mistake when he wrongly assumed that the Confederates had penetrated his lines and pulled troops from other points to reinforce the perceived breakthrough. The shifting of troops created a weak point in the Federal lines and Confederate General James Longstreet, assigned to Bragg on temporary duty from the Army of Northern Virginia, sent his troops smashing through the gap. Rosecrans, forced to flee the battlefield with approximately one-half the Federal army, concentrated his forces in Chattanooga, while Major General George H. Thomas assumed command of the remaining Federals left on the field. Consolidating his troops along a line on Snodgrass Hill, Thomas effectively defended his position throughout the day, withdrawing only after darkness had fallen.

Throughout the battle, Florida troops were disciplined and courageous. Not only had the First, Third, and Fourth Regiments performed well, but the previously untried Sixth and Seventh Regiments were equally impressive in their engagements. So, too, were the men of the Florida First Cavalry Regiment and those of the Florida Marion Artillery, under the command of Captain John M. Martin.

The cost had been high, however. Colonel William S. Dilworth, the commander of the Florida First and Third, which had been consolidated previously, reported 92 men out of a total of 273 were killed, wounded, or missing—a casualty rate of 34 percent. Colonel Wiles L.L. Bowen, who led the Florida Fourth, reported the loss of 87 men. The Sixth Florida, commanded by Colonel Jesse J. Finley, reported its losses as 35 killed and 130 wounded. Only the Florida Seventh escaped major losses during the battle. As a result of these losses, all Florida regiments, including the First Regiment of Florida Cavalry, were consolidated into a single brigade under the command of Finley, who had been promoted to brigadier general, and assigned to the division commanded by Brigadier William B. Bate.

Thomas's withdrawal into Chattanooga left the Confederates in control of the battlefield and gave them a decided victory. Federal troops were now at the mercy of

LEFT: *John Marshall Martin, later colonel of the Ninth Florida Infantry, commanded the Florida Marion Artillery during the Battle of Chattanooga. (Florida State Archives.)*
RIGHT: *Colonel Jesse J. Finley was part of the Sixth Florida Infantry Regiment. (Museum of the Confederacy.)*

Bragg's army that occupied the heights overlooking the city and from which Confederate artillery denied them the supplies they needed to feed and replenish the army. Just months after the Union had successfully laid siege to Vicksburg, it found itself in much the same position at Chattanooga—an entire Federal army unable to sustain itself—an unacceptable situation.

The Union loss at Chickamauga was a decisive moment for the Federal government. After its earlier successes in 1863, this setback demanded and received immediate attention. Aware that inaction would ultimately result in the loss of Rosecrans's army, Union authorities ordered Major General Joseph Hooker to move his army of 20,000 to Chattanooga immediately. Major General William Tecumseh Sherman arrived from Mississippi with an army of 16,000 in mid-October. General Ulysses S. Grant was placed in overall command of the situation. General Rosecrans, who had triumphed just months earlier at Murfreesboro and Tullahoma, lost his command to General Thomas.

The arrival of the additional Federal troops under the steady command of Grant tilted the balance of power from Bragg to the Union. Immediately after his arrival, Grant managed to break the siege of Chattanooga by securing a short supply line from Alabama. Now able to provide food and ammunition for all of his army, he developed plans to oust Bragg's forces from the heights surrounding the city.

On November 23, Major General Thomas attacked Confederate positions on Orchard Knob and forced their evacuation. The next day, Hooker's army routed Confederate troops on the slopes of Lookout Mountain. On November 25, Grant launched Sherman's army against the Confederates, who were now concentrated on Missionary Ridge. When Sherman's attack was halted by the strong defensive positions on the ridge, Grant then dispatched Hooker to attack the Confederate left. Thomas's men, who had been held in reserve at the center of the Union line, were ordered to assault the Southern rifle pits at the base of Missionary Ridge. Quickly accomplishing this feat, they continued up the ridge against the entrenched Confederates. The quick assault by Thomas collapsed the Southern defenses, and Bragg's troops quickly retreated.

The failure of Bragg to first hold and then retake Chattanooga was a critical turning point in the war. Although both armies went immediately into winter quarters—Grant in Chattanooga and Bragg in north Georgia—changes were occurring that would dictate the outcome of the conflict. Ulysses S. Grant, having successfully dealt with Bragg, was now transferred to Virginia and placed in overall command of Union armies. Sherman, a longtime associate of Grant, was given command of the Federal army poised to attack the heart of the Confederacy through Georgia.

For Bragg, failure at Chattanooga meant the end of his career as an active battlefield commander. Confederate soldiers no longer had confidence in his abilities as a general, and the rumblings of discontent were heard in Richmond. President Jefferson Davis relieved Bragg of his command and replaced him with General Joseph E. Johnston. Bragg was called to the Confederate capital to serve as Davis's military advisor.

*This is a post-war photograph of Missionary Ridge. Such photographs were popular with both Union and Confederate veterans and were frequently sold as part of the many "memory" books that were published.*

*John Bell Hood was a courageous soldier, but most of the common soldiers in the Army of Tennessee considered him to be rash and foolhardy. He was not a popular commander when he replaced Joseph E. Johnston in 1864. (National Archives.)*

Florida troops had paid a high price during the Chattanooga campaign. The main part of Florida Brigade had been stationed at the center of the Confederate lines at the beginning of the battle of Missionary Ridge, but soon units of the Florida First, Fourth, and Seventh were detailed to duty in the rifle pits at the bottom of the ridge and in skirmish positions on the valley floor. During the battle, the Florida Fourth lost 154 of 172 men killed or wounded. The other units suffered similar casualties. General Bate, in his after battle report, placed his losses at 43 soldiers killed, 224 wounded, and 590 missing. "Most of the latter," he continued, "were Floridians who were in the trenches."

When Sherman launched his move toward Atlanta in the spring of 1864, the Florida brigade was in the thick of the fighting as Joseph E. Johnston successfully delayed the advance of the Federal army. From the initial battle at Dalton on May 7, 1864, through the evacuation of Atlanta on September 1, the Florida brigade participated in each of the battles—Dalton, Rocky Face, Resaca, Calhoun, Adairsville, Cassville, Acworth, Kenesaw Mountain, Cheatham Hill, Peachtree Creek, Utoy Creek, and Jonesboro. When the Confederate army, now under the command of Major General John Bell Hood, moved north out of the Atlanta area, the brigade moved with it, covering the same ground that had only months before been sacrificed at such a heavy cost.

As Hood moved north, Sherman continued southward across Georgia and reached Savannah on December 22. Hood continued his movement north and, on November 30,

*Major General William Tecumseh Sherman was placed in command of Union forces in the west after the Battle of Missionary Ridge. (*Leslie's Illustrated Newspaper.*)*

assaulted Federal forces at Franklin, Tennessee. In a pyrrhic victory in which the Army of Tennessee suffered some 6,000 casualties, Hood forced the Union army to retreat to Nashville, where the Union army settled behind prepared defenses. The Battle of Franklin had cost the Confederates fully one-third of their combat effectives. Union casualties were less than one-half of those suffered by the Confederates.

Ignoring the tremendous losses of the previous day, Hood pursued the Union army to Nashville. Despite facing an army almost twice the size of his own, Hood laid siege to Nashville. The two armies faced each other across their reinforced lines. Hood, now commanding a force weakened by the continuous fighting of the Atlanta campaign, the constant marching in the aftermath of the loss of that city, and the horrific casualties at Franklin, had little opportunity to do more than wait for the Union army to come to him.

In Nashville, George H. Thomas, the Union commander, realized that Hood, though limited in his ability to strike, commanded an army that was still capable of delivering a devastating blow. Authorities in Washington, embarrassed by the possibility of Hood crossing the Ohio River and invading Northern territory, urged Thomas to attack immediately, but Thomas delayed moving against Hood until such time as cavalry units could reinforce him. From Virginia, Ulysses S. Grant, the field commander of all Union armies, urged that Thomas be replaced by another, more aggressive commander. For more than a week, Thomas refused to move. When he did decide to begin his attack on Hood on December 11, the Nashville area was hit by a major ice storm, which further delayed any offensive movement by the Federal army. Exasperated, Grant ordered General John A. Logan to relieve Thomas and made plans to go to Nashville himself. Before Logan could reach Nashville, Thomas unleashed a lumbering, but overwhelming, attack against Hood on December 15. More than 50,000 Federal troops pounded the defenses manned by less than 20,000 Confederate soldiers. For two days, the Southern army exacted a heavy toll from its attackers but faced certain defeat. On December 17, Hood ordered the Army of Tennessee to retreat.

The battle at Nashville was the last important conflict fought by the Army of Tennessee. Although Southern casualties had been relatively light (1,500) compared to those suffered by the Union army (3,061), the Confederate army had been constantly engaged in fighting since May. It was exhausted, but more importantly, the Confederacy had been drained of manpower and resources to such an extent that replacements for men and materiel was impossible. Although still capable of inflicting great damage, particularly in a defensive engagement, the Army of Tennessee had blunted its offensive capabilities in front of Nashville.

Leaving Nashville, Hood led his army toward relative safety in Mississippi. Pursued by Federal cavalry detachments, the army fought several small skirmishes throughout December until it crossed the Tennessee River at Bainbridge on the December 27. For the Army of Tennessee and the Confederacy, the death-knell had been sounded, but the war was not over.

*William J. Hardee commanded Confederate forces in Savannah and evacuated that city when Sherman's army approached.*

The year 1865 began with the knowledge that the Confederacy was living on borrowed time. In Virginia, General Ulysses S. Grant and a Union army of 110,000 soldiers were hammering on the doors of Petersburg, while Confederate General Robert E. Lee tried desperately to defend the city with a force of only 65,000. In Georgia, General William Tecumseh Sherman began his operations against Confederate General William J. Hardee by transferring troops from Savannah to Beaufort, South Carolina.

In Mississippi, the reduced Army of Tennessee began preparations to move eastward to assist Hardee against Sherman. On January 7, John Bell Hood resigned his command of the army and was replaced on an interim basis by Lieutenant General Richard Taylor, under the supervision of P.G.T. Beauregard, who was in overall command of Confederate operations in the Carolinas. Hood's departure was welcomed by most of the soldiers who firmly believed that he had frittered away the strength of the army with futile attacks against Sherman during the battle for Atlanta. With Hood's resignation, the Army of Tennessee completed its movement to South Carolina.

On February 17, the army participated in the skirmishing outside Columbia, but no major battle developed. On February 22, Joseph E. Johnston, the army's former commander during the Atlanta campaign, was brought out of retirement and given command of the remnants of this once mighty force. Johnston's objective was to prevent Sherman from joining Grant in Virginia and from further dividing the Confederacy. Johnston hoped to place himself and his army of 20,000 in such a position that the Army of Tennessee would be able to hold Sherman at bay, while opening lines of transportation between his forces and the 60,000 men of Robert E. Lee in Virginia. This would allow Confederate troops to be shuttled between both armies on an "as needed" basis, effectively strengthening both armies.

Sherman was not about to allow this to happen. Collecting Union forces from throughout the Carolinas, he soon had a force of approximately 100,000 men to draw on. On March 18, forward units of Confederate cavalry clashed with advance units of the Federal army moving toward Goldsborough, North Carolina. By early the next morning, Johnston and the Army of Tennessee were fully involved in a major confrontation with Sherman's forces in the vicinity of Bentonville. For three days, the Army of Tennessee attempted to deliver a fatal blow to the Union army. Despite inflicting far more casualties (3,000) than they received (1,500), the Confederates could not halt the numerically superior Federal force and were forced to withdraw.

Realizing that the Army of Tennessee could not defeat the Union forces opposing it, Johnston placed his remaining forces astraddle the major roads leading into Virginia. Here he hoped to delay Federal forces moving to join with Grant at Petersburg and to provide Lee with an opportunity to combine forces after Petersburg fell. When that city and Richmond fell on April 3, Johnston prepared his army for a union with that of Lee.

By April 7, it was apparent that Lee would not be able to escape from Grant in Virginia, and, on April 9, Lee surrendered at Appomattox Courthouse. That same day, Johnston reorganized the Army of Tennessee in an effort to continue the Confederate war effort. All Florida units were consolidated into a single regiment, the First Florida, and placed under the command of Lieutenant Elisha Mashburn.

In other theaters, Confederate fortunes were also suffering greatly. Mobile, under assault by a Union army, surrendered on April 12. Charleston Harbor saw the United States flag raised over Fort Sumter by General Robert Anderson, who had lowered it four years earlier. Perhaps, however, the greatest blow to the Confederacy came with the shooting of Abraham Lincoln on the same day. His death on April 15 incensed the North and gave pause to remaining Confederate forces still operating.

Realizing the futility of further resistance, Confederate President Jefferson Davis authorized Joseph E. Johnston to begin negotiations for the surrender of the Army of Tennessee. On April 18, Johnston signed an agreement with William T. Sherman that effectively ended the Confederate experiment. Although minor skirmishing would continue for several days, the war was over.

Although exact casualty figures are not available for each Florida regiment in each battle fought in the western theater, the losses suffered by the Fourth might be considered typical. When the regiment was organized in June 1862, it was composed of 926 enlisted men and 47 officers. When it surrendered in late April 1865, there were only 23 men left. Not all of the losses were battle-related deaths, however. Like all Civil war soldiers, Floridians fell prey to malaria, dysentery, and a host of other diseases. Some soldiers were captured and interned in Federal prison camps; still others were wounded and sent home, while unsanitary conditions of army hospitals claimed many more in the days and months after they were wounded. Finally, some Floridians, faced with the prospect of death or the harsh demands of army life, deserted their units.

In the main, however, Florida units attached to the Army of Tennessee had served faithfully and bravely for almost four years. They left a record of soldierly achievement with which they could be proud.

# 5. INSIDE THE CONFEDERATE STOREHOUSE

As the Confederacy battled with the Union during the Civil War both sides quickly learned the ancient lesson of war that logistics was crucial to their respective war efforts. While neither glamorous nor heroic, supplying troops with food, clothing, and ammunition in adequate amounts often made the difference between victory and defeat. Finding ways to make certain that sufficient goods were in the right place at the right time became a major challenge to Johnny Reb and Billy Yank alike. Officers in blue or gray constantly pushed and prodded their men in this—at times—thankless task of gathering the sinews of war.

The Confederate states faced huge obstacles in meeting this supply challenge, most of which its leaders did not contemplate before the firing on Fort Sumter. The new nation was mainly agricultural, and non-edible cotton remained king. Its industrial base was miniscule compared to that of the North, though wartime manufacturing would work near miracles in producing needed items. The region's transportation system was inadequate for wartime traffic, especially the South's underdeveloped and incomplete railroad system. As the struggle dragged on it became very clear to rebel quartermasters and commissary officers that if the Confederacy was to prevail it must organize and utilize its resources to fuel its war machine or face the hard consequences. All the states would have to contribute to their fullest despite the hindering consideration of states rights. Failure to do so would cripple the Confederate army to a greater degree than the enemy ever could.

Ironically, Florida, which the Richmond government had all but abandoned to the Federals, stepped forward to become a key component of the Southern war economy. Its antebellum reputation as an agricultural powerhouse followed it out of the Union and soon the Confederate government would expect much from it in terms of supplies. It continually placed more and more demands on the peninsula state for sustenance. However, many of these same officials never had a realistic notion of just what Florida could supply and the massive problems of getting such materials out of the state and to the troops that needed them. Even as the war progressed supply bureaucrats constantly

*The railroad systems of the South were small and inefficient compared to those of the North. In Florida, the major railroad linking the east and west coasts at Fernandina and Cedar Key was only completed in March 1861. (Contemporary print.)*

made demands bordering on the fantastic from isolated, frontier Florida. Bemused Floridians labored hard in the midst of serious trials to meet at least some of these requests.

Transportation greatly hampered Florida's ability to funnel goods northward to the rest of the Confederacy. With the coming of the Union naval blockade the network of coastal vessels that previously linked state ports with Mobile, New Orleans, Savannah, and Charleston ground slowly to a halt. Florida's river system was used to its utmost, especially the St. Johns and the Apalachicola, but most were too shallow or ran in the wrong directions to meet military needs. Most streams would see rafts bearing cotton, turpentine, and other goods floating down to the Gulf of Mexico or the Atlantic coast for waiting blockade-runners. In time these same rivers would enable Union forces sailing in small boats to push into the interior in search of economic targets worth putting to the torch.

Land transportation in the state offered even less. No major roads ran through Florida in the 1860s, and those that did exist were little better than sandy tracks with small load-bearing capacity. Many were glorified wagon trails that made for rough going even under the best of conditions. Hauling heavy cargoes along them was all but impossible, thus the dependence on water transportation. Pre-war Florida travel accounts told tales of a brave few pressing on in the face of scorching heat, unrelenting insects, poisonous snakes, and, of course, bandits and bushwhackers of all varieties. A trip from the shores of Lake Okeechobee to the border with Georgia could last as long as 30 difficult days.

The answer to this Florida problem was formulated in the late 1850s and was the same solution other Southern states craved. A mania for railroad construction gripped the region and Floridians soon longed for the sound of steam engines running through the piney woods. Three major rail lines ran through Florida by the coming of the Civil War, the first pushing north from Pensacola to just beyond the Alabama state line. A second linked Jacksonville to Tallahassee, with a trunk line stretching down to St. Marks on the Gulf. Lastly, the Florida Railroad connected Fernandina with Cedar Key and could boast of being the largest line operating in Florida by 1861. Unfortunately, all of these lines proved unable to continue moving at anywhere near pre-war capacity, and during the conflict some had to fight to protect the very rails their trains ran on from being confiscated by the Confederate government and used to augment existing tracks in other states. Also surprisingly there was no direct connection with Georgia's extensive railroad system. By the time iron tracks linking Live Oak and Lawton, Georgia, were hammered into place in 1865, it was far too late to be of any major service.

Any and all transportation was necessary as the war progressed and armies grew to record numbers of soldiers. Mountains of bulky army rations had to be procured and moved to distribution points near the front lines every day whether there was fighting or not. Agricultural products rose in price and grew increasingly scarce for troops and civilians alike. Without refrigeration perishable meats had to be salted before shipment. Ordinary salt was used to preserve such materials in the antebellum South, especially pork

*The United States Navy used a variety of ships and small boats to enforce its blockade of the Southern coasts. (Contemporary print.)*

*Salt production was critical to the Confederacy's military, industrial, and civilian communities. Producing salt from saltwater was relatively easy, but salt works were easy targets for Union raiders from the blockading squadrons. (*Leslie's Illustrated Newspaper.*)*

products, and was an important ingredient in tanning leather. High-quality imported foreign salt flooded into the region before 1861, and local sources were deemed more than sufficient to meet demand. However, overseas salt deliveries all but ended with the outbreak of war and the coming of the blockade just as government orders for it skyrocketed. By the end of the year the entire Confederacy was in the grips of a salt shortage the likes of which it had never seen before. Even Floridians ran short and had to take steps like recovering salt from the earthen floors of smoke houses. A salt plant did exist in Key West, but Union occupiers shut it down so as not to supply the rebels with its saline. Something dramatic had to be done or the South might lose its bid for independence due to a lack of sodium chloride.

Florida natives and other Southerners soon turned to salt water to ease their salt famine. Briny water from the Atlantic, the Gulf, or salty wetlands could be refined into usable salt crystals with a minimum of equipment and effort. All that was really required was the water itself, some sort of vessel to boil it in, and amounts of firewood for fuel. In short order, old sugar kettles or metal harbor buoys were pressed into service as boilers on Florida's coastlines. Soon boiling operations large and small were processing enough salt to meet local needs and soon a surplus for export to other salt-starved states. Salt workers soon received praise for their patriotic labors for the cause, while they themselves enjoyed the substantial profits from their work as well as an exemption from the Confederate military draft.

*Because salt works were usually located in marshy areas near the ocean or bays, workers had to find ways to defeat the hordes of mosquitoes that swarmed in the hot Florida climate. Here workers have buried themselves in sand to keep the buzzing pests at bay. (Contemporary print.)*

By the end of 1862 Florida was shipping large quantities of usable salt into both Georgia and Alabama. This helped to feed demand and stop the upward spiral of prices. Wartime salt-making became a big business from what had once been a tiny antebellum enterprise. The Confederacy certainly could not do without it, and this shows the impact of the Civil War on non-agricultural economic activities. In time salt-boiling complexes sprang up using large custom-designed boilers and ceramic-lined drying pans. These plants employed hundreds of workers and soon many slaves whose masters wanted them to learn the valuable trade. By war's end Florida's production of salt would prove to be it greatest contribution in terms of monetary value to the Confederate economy.

The highest concentration of salt-boiling operations in Florida during the Civil War was on the shores of St. Andrews Bay in Washington County in the Panhandle. Unlimited salt water, plentiful pine trees for fuel, and several wagon trails leading away from the coast made this a prime area for such efforts. Its geography even helped, as Union forces offshore could not approach the bays and inlets without being detected well in advance. But at night sailors on the decks of Federal warships out in the Gulf could see the glow of many boiler fires and smell the peculiar odor of boiling salt water. Knowing how valuable such works were to the rebel armies, these men yearned to get ashore and smash them to bits.

Destroying the salt plants, however, proved to be a frustrating chore for the Union sailors and marines involved. Landing parties often rowed ashore along the beaches in search of salt works to eliminate. The Yankees then sweated under the sun as they swung axes and sledgehammers against boilers and kettles or threw bags of finished salt back into the sea. They burned shelters and wagons used in the trade and encouraged slave workers to leave and join the Union as "contrabands of war." Many African-American bondservants laboring on the coasts in this manner took the opportunity for freedom and left with the sailors. Few of these raids met armed resistance, and most salt-boilers took to their heels, and to the woods, well before the Federals arrived. Despite these strenuous efforts the Unionists only slowed production of salt but never stopped it. Without troops to permanently occupy the salt areas like St. Andrews Bay, Northern forces could only impede salt manufacturing in wartime Florida and not halt it. Many of these plants continued operating well past the end of hostilities in 1865.

Florida farmers toiled as diligently as salt makers to aid the Southern cause and frequently faced many of the same challenges. Middle Florida cotton growers felt the pressure to convert to food crops to feed the armies and help create a major cotton famine that might convince Great Britain and France to intervene in the struggle. Despite considerable governmental and public demands to the contrary cotton continued to bloom in the state during the war. Its value as a cash crop remained high, and planters argued that, if nothing else, they needed a fresh supply of cottonseeds for cultivation when

*Slaves were considered contrabands of war. Whenever the Union army or navy was reported to be near, some slaves left the plantations and made their way toward the Federal troops. (Library of Congress.)*

the war ended. Probably the lure of large profits from running heavy bales out through the Union blockade was just too tempting for all Florida agriculturalists to resist.

Emphasis on staple crops like corn, capable of feeding men and animals, was redoubled as the struggle progressed. By 1862 Florida corn found its way to markets in Georgia to help ease a serious grain shortage all across the lower South. Local corn yields began to fall the next year, and by 1864, Floridians themselves faced a critical corn and grain shortage. Despite its reputation as the "granary" or "garden farm" of the Confederacy, Florida growers could never keep up with increasing demands for corn and balked at selling their maize for inflated Confederate currency of dubious value. They liked even less the idea of having it impressed by government quartermasters in return for promises. Rich harvests had turned to poor ones by 1865, and many Florida residents learned to endure the pangs of hunger as a result.

One reason for wartime corn shortages was the common practice of distilling and selling Florida corn in the form of corn whisky. By 1862 the state legislature had banned private whisky making without a permit, but such an edict hardly slowed this traditional rural practice. Ironically, the Confederate States Navy and Surgeon General's Office were the biggest buyers of Florida-brewed corn liquor. Need soared after every battle, as rebel physicians usually had little else to offer the wounded in field hospitals to ease the pain of their injuries. For example, whiskey from Florida went northward to depots in Augusta in 1864 for distribution among Confederate regiments fighting to hold back the advance of General William T. Sherman's bluecoats toward Atlanta.

The thousands of sick rebel soldiers also looked to Florida citrus groves for fruits that might speed their recovery. Doctors sought oranges, lemons, and limes from the early days of the conflict, and these helped in no small way to revive what had been a flagging industry. Even occupying Union troopers took a fancy to fresh citrus fruit hanging free for the taking from local trees. Many even managed to ship whole boxes of oranges northward by express company to grace family tables or make welcome Christmas presents. Thus began a tradition for Florida visitors that continues to this day and helped re-energize the state's citrus growers and make it one of the pillars of Florida agriculture.

Probably the most important foodstuff supplied by Florida during the Civil War was beef cattle. The state enjoyed a serious antebellum reputation as cattle country, and many natives boasted that Florida might even best Texas in beef production. They would point with some pride to the fact that the American cattle industry was born on the Florida peninsula in the 16th century. Spanish explorers brought cowherds along during their expeditions for food and a few escaped to thrive in the wild. By 1860 South Florida was to be the home of many large herds of semi-wild bovines annually rounded up and driven to market. Tough "cracker" cowmen worked these herds and many grew into ranchers owning thousands of head. Very few realized that the coming of civil war would threaten their isolated way of life.

After the firing on Fort Sumter the Confederate government began letting out contracts to cattle men in Florida to supply the growing rebel armies with beef. One of the first to enter this new trade was legendary veteran cowman Jacob Summerlin. "Uncle Jake" had been one of the pioneers of the beef trade between Florida and the Spanish island of Cuba in partnership with Tampa's James McKay. Summerlin soon had cows trudging toward

*Jacob Summerlin sold cattle to the Confederacy during the war. He continued his occupation in the postwar period. (Florida State Archives.)*

Georgia and South Carolina by the thousands. The 30-day cattle drive was a test for both men and animals, with stops at rallying points like Payne's Prairie to the south of Gainesville. Prices paid at the end of the trail ranged from $8 to $10 per head depending on condition. However, the dollars remitted to Summerlin and his drovers were Confederate ones, and all were a bit uneasy at selling their precious herds for currency of uncertain value.

As 1863 dawned, Summerlin and company began to express dissatisfaction with their business arrangement with the Richmond government. Summerlin and McKay turned their attention to smuggling cattle down to Cuba in return for Spanish gold and other blockade-running opportunities. They made isolated Punta Rassa on the southwest Gulf coast a center for their operations. In short order the contractor system fell by the wayside and left the government without cattle suppliers. Very few were willing to put patriotism above potential profits and their own futures. Most grumbled that the Confederacy had done precious little for them and just might not survive its war for independence.

The news of 1863 seemed to confirm these Floridians' suspicions of the Confederate States' chances. By mid-July Robert E. Lee's Army of Northern Virginia, including Florida troops, fought and lost the battle of Gettysburg. Lee's army would never really recover from the defeat in Pennsylvania. At almost the same time to the west General U.S. Grant had finally forced the 30,000-man garrison of Vicksburg to lay down their weapons. With Vicksburg and soon Port Hudson the Union now had full control of the Mississippi River and effectively sliced the Confederacy in two. This successfully denied access to the supply-rich areas west of the mighty river. Confederate Commissary-General Lucius B. Northrop, an intimate of President Jefferson Davis, and other supply officials now faced the hard fact that theirs was to be a long, protracted war waged with an ever-shrinking base to support it. Each remaining state, Florida in particular, must be combed for needed articles or the cause could indeed become a lost one.

Under earlier pressure to better feed the armies, Commissary-General Northrop unveiled a new supply-gathering system on April 15. Each rebel state was to have its own head commissary officer to directly supervise the collection and transportation of all food supplies. This officer had the authority to deal with Richmond and quartermasters from the Confederate armies themselves. He could also sub-divide his state into as many districts as he saw fit to help facilitate this vital mission. Northrop hoped that new arrangement would better meet supply needs and deflect some of the heavy criticism he and his office had received from army commanders.

Florida moved quickly to conform to the new Northrop supply system. An administrator of no mean ability was essential to handle what was doubtlessly a difficult task. Quincy resident Pleasants W. White, a leading attorney and ardent Confederate, donned a major's uniform and went to work to transform the new plan from a paper idea to a working reality. Almost immediately he knew that a state the size of Florida would have to be divided into smaller more manageable regions. Some five commissary districts

LEFT: *Commissary-General Lucius B. Northrop, CSA. (Artwork by Jeanette Boughner.)*
RIGHT: *Pleasants Woodson White, Florida's commissary-general. (Pleasants W. White Collection, Tebeau-Field Library of Florida History.)*

would in time be created with officers or civilian heads to run them. The Fifth District encompassed the cattle-rich southern counties of Hernando, Hillsborough, Manatee, Polk, Brevard, Dade, and Monroe and was perhaps the most crucial of all. White tapped James McKay, an experienced cattle dealer and Tampa civic leader, to command the district.

McKay himself had already endured much since 1861, including imprisonment when his ship the *Salvor* was captured while attempting to run the Union blockade. The Scot won his release but continued to enjoy a shadowy relationship with Federal authorities. Historians have even alleged that he may have defected to the Yankees with the promise of cutting off shipments of south Florida beef to the rebels. While records are sketchy and the evidence is far from complete, Major White had enough confidence to appoint McKay and keep him at this essential post until the end in 1865. If McKay's covert mission was to disrupt the cattle drives from the southern half of the Florida peninsula, he failed to accomplish it.

The new supply scheme was far from perfect and allowed for too much competition among various military and civilian groups. Such wasted effort could be ill afforded by a Confederacy battling for its life against a strong and determined opponent. But by the end of August 1863, herds of record sizes did leave the state to feed troops in the hard-luck Army of Tennessee and the hard-pressed garrison at Charleston. However, the army's stated requests for 3,000 head per week was never met and was nowhere near being a realistic goal. Major White expended much paper and ink in vain attempts to explain to supply bureaucrats what was and was not possible from his Florida operation. Despite his efforts the major never made his colleagues understand the hard facts of gathering and moving supplies in Florida.

The arrival of winter in late 1863 meant another lean season of scanty rations for Confederate troops whether they were in Virginia or the hills of north Georgia. Under stress to procure food, White issued a frank appeal in the form of a written circular to the leading citizens of Florida asking for their help. He pleaded for their assistance to meet urgent ration requests, especially for beef cattle. White reported the gravity of the situation in the army camps and supported his case with direct quotes from military messages from the front begging for supplies. He asserted in his paper that the people of Florida must "support the soldiers or the South is lost." White meant that his report be read only by state leaders, but the secret document soon became common knowledge among the general populace. The White Circular plainly showed how important Florida had become to the Southern war effort.

The vital need for Florida beef increased in early 1864, as did the difficulties of getting it for the government. Confederate draft-dodgers and deserters now lurked in many parts of South Florida and raided cattle herds for food at will. The old Seminole War post Fort Myers sprang back to life when seized by Federal forces in the previous December and played host to Unionists striking into the interior. Government policies like the Impressment Act caused many a South Florida rancher to hide his bovines in the piney wilderness rather than lose them to agents that paid far too little for them or nothing at all. Of course, the reports from the fighting fronts told tales of starvation-like conditions in many Confederate units.

*Charles James Munnerlyn was part of the First Florida "Cow Cavalry." (Georgia State Archives.)*

Florida's role as a supply source and its general military weakness could not be denied when Federal troops began a major advance into the northeastern corner of the state that ended with the clash at Olustee on February 20, 1864. The Yankee objectives in the Olustee campaign had been to sever the flow of foodstuffs and other supplies from Florida into the hands of rebels defending Charleston, South Carolina. Supply lines were indeed cut or disrupted for several weeks after the unsuccessful Union attack at Olustee, adding to the ongoing privations of Johnny Reb.

Some sort of decisive action had to be taken to get the beef and other edibles moving again. A proposal from James McKay at about that time seemed to have great promise. He wanted to organize a special battalion of mounted troops whose primary mission would be gathering the wild cows and protecting them on their way to Georgia. Local men who knew the ranges and how to work those animals were a must in McKay's mind. The cattle battalion, or "Cow Cavalry," secured the waiting herds while at the same time showing the people of South Florida that the Confederate government cared for their safety and wanted stability and order in the region. Volunteers for the companies that composed the battalion came from residents or men with cattle experience detailed from the regular army for this key task. Even men with little allegiance to the Confederacy came forward and enlisted in the "Cow Cavalry" to protect their homes and families, as well as their herds, from marauders of all stripes.

Companies formed in South and Central Florida under the command of ex-Georgia congressman Charles J. Munnerlyn. Almost at once the presence of these horsemen on the trails brought a degree of calm to the entire region they patrolled. Beef deliveries to government agents increased and became more regular with their help. Regular army officers continually bemoaned their lack of spit-and-polish discipline, but locals cheered their arrival with gusto. At least one senior officer, General James Patton Anderson, wanted as many men stripped from cattle operations in Florida as possible and sent to the fighting fronts. Richmond officials almost disbanded the "Cow Cavalry" as a result, though ardent objections from citizens and supply officers ended the idea.

While Munnerlyn's battalion fought to provide meat to their comrades facing the Yankees and for their own existence as a unit, Union prisoners of war held in Georgia struggled to simply live from day to day. By June 1864 the population of the infamous Andersonville prison had reached a staggering 26,000 inmates, and rations for them were in very short supply. Officials there begged Major White for any surplus food items that Florida could spare. Compassionately, the Floridian ordered some 1,700 head of cattle transferred to the camp as soon as possible. Little else besides some kegs of molasses made it across the state line to the starving Federals. Unfortunately, the human tragedy that was Andersonville continued.

The winter of 1864–1865 saw another cold and hungry time for Southern soldiers and many of their families at home. Florida had offered what it could, but expectations still remained unrealistically high that the state still held large untapped sources of supply. Even though senior officers like Commissary-General Northrop knew and reported such tales of huge herds grazing in South Florida as pure fantasy, others continued to believe otherwise. A saddened Major White asked in a December 1864 letter "what is to be the fate of our armies, now almost solidly dependent upon our state for meat. Heaven only knows."

*Francis Asbury Hendry, surrounded here by Seminole Indian chiefs, was a captain in the First Florida Cow Cavalry. (Florida State Archives.)*

*This is an aerial view of Andersonville Prison where thousands of Federal prisoners died from starvation and unsanitary conditions. Captain Henry Wirz, the prison commandant, was hanged at the end of the war. (Contemporary print.)*

By the bleak spring even those few military units stationed in Florida itself were on scanty and inadequate rations. But those shivering in the trenches around Petersburg in Virginia suffered even greater pangs of hunger. Almost every night tattered rebel soldiers there voted with their feet on the Confederacy's chances and went over to the Federals. Criticism of the supply bureaus reached such a point that even President Davis could not shield his old friend Commissary-General Northrop. In February he was removed from his office and replaced with Isaac M. Saint John, but in the end it made little difference. Despite all the efforts in Florida and the other Confederate states, the South had failed to amply feed its troops. This along with other factors slowly sapped their will to resist and sank morale. To many, even defeat seemed a better option than the continual suffering of themselves and their loved ones waiting at home. By the first warmth of spring in 1865 the Confederacy began to disintegrate, but some sections managed to hold out a bit longer in the face of general collapse.

This was the case with supply operations in Florida. The 1865 cattle-driving season commenced in April, and White believed that with work some 10,000 to 15,000 head might yet be had for the Richmond government. Of course the fall of Richmond and the scattering of the Confederate government made such deliveries impossible. Plans were even in the works to slaughter beef, pack it in heavy salt, and ship it by boat up the Apalachicola River to Columbus, and from there to Macon for distribution. But again events to the north at Appomattox Court House cancelled such schemes. As word of Lee's surrender reached Florida troops they instinctively knew the war was over and many slipped away from the ranks to head for home. By summer Union forces controlled

Tallahassee and fanned out into the interior of the state to take the surrenders of any rebels forces still in existence. By June all Confederate troops had laid down their arms and most had accepted parole from the victorious Yankees, which included taking an oath to obey the laws of the United States. Even as the ink dried on these parole forms, warehouses in various parts of the state were still filled to capacity with stores of supplies that were the property of the now defunct rebel government.

Returning veterans faced the uncertain task of making a living in an area whose economy had been all but shattered by the Civil War. But all was not doom and gloom. The cattle trade with Cuba would soon return, as would the citrus and lumber industries. Union veterans who had admired Florida's beauty during the war yearned to return to the peninsula with money to invest in these businesses. Those that did brought the necessary capital to start a post-war economy. Florida was fortunate that the damage it suffered during the conflict was small when compared to the havoc inflicted in states like Georgia, South Carolina, or Virginia.

Florida had indeed been a Confederate storehouse during the War between the States. Very significant quantities of cattle, pork, salt, corn, citrus fruit, and other commodities went into the hands of the Confederate government. This aided in no small way the South's ability to keep armies in the field and fighting. Richmond, though it never really understood Florida's logistical limitations, continued to place demands upon it for sustenance that could never be met. The state deserves much credit for all that it did do to provide supplies in the face of Union attacks and a divided and increasingly war-weary population at home. That Florida's frontier society could face the threats of Unionists and raiders of all types with such a large percentage of its men away in the army and still be such a provider says much about the stoic fiber of these pioneers. Florida was an essential economic member of the Confederate States of America and historians have only recently given it the credit that it is due.

# 6. Enduring the Blockade

On April 19, 1861, President Abraham Lincoln and his advisors made a momentous decision to blockade the entire coastline of the Confederate States. Although the United States Navy had only 35 vessels when the war broke out, only 3 of which were steam powered, a major portion of the nation's resources were devoted to implementing this policy. The impact of this policy on the U.S. war effort was both positive and enormous. Indeed, it is very unlikely that the war could have been successfully concluded in its favor had this policy not been integrated in the overall strategy of the United States.

The naval blockade was both daring and dangerous for the United States, and, in order to impose it effectively, the nation had to ignore existing international laws. Although other nations had imposed similar blockades in the past, the proposal of the United States differed in several ways from the previous efforts. Prevailing international law concerning naval blockades, which had been formalized in the Declaration of Paris in 1856, stipulated that such blockades "in order to be binding, must be effective—that is to say, maintained by a force sufficient to prevent access to the coast of the enemy." In addition, the declaration also specified that the blockading power could capture or confiscate only "contraband of war" and that other goods were protected from confiscation. Last, the declaration limited blockades to warring parties.

The United States was not a signatory of the Declaration of Paris and, as a result, chose to ignore the broad outlines of the declaration and established new policies for blockades. First, the United States created the blockade despite the fact that it never recognized the legitimacy of the Confederate States of America and therefore was never technically at war with it. Throughout the Civil War, the policy of the United States was that the fighting with the Confederacy amounted to a "civil insurrection," not a war. In all of its diplomatic correspondence and official statements, the Federal government insisted that it was fighting a "rebellion," not a war. This bit of verbal gymnastics created potential conflicts with other nations who questioned the validity of the blockade, but, within three years, the Union navy was the largest naval force in the world. In a case where might truly did make right, there was nothing that other countries could do to change U.S. policy.

The imposition and maintenance of the naval blockade in the Civil War re-wrote international law, and, in the early 1900s, this precedent was one of the justifications used by Theodore Roosevelt in establishing his "Big Stick" policy in the Western Hemisphere.

Second, despite its initial inability to maintain the blockade "by a force sufficient to prevent access to the coast of the enemy," the United States proceeded to act as if the blockade was absolute. Ignoring the protests of neutral nations and their claims for confiscated cargoes, the United States resolved to answer those questions after the war had been won. Third, the declaration also outlawed privateering, but during the war, the United States supported a form of "semi-privateering" by distributing the monies received from the sale of captured ships and confiscated cargoes among the officers and sailors of the naval vessels that had captured them. Last, the Declaration of Paris stipulated that the only goods that could be legally confiscated were those that were "contraband of war." In enforcing the blockade, the United States declared that all goods, whether they had a specific military use or not, would be seized. This included goods and cargoes sent out of the Confederate states, as well as those coming in. The purpose of the Federal blockade was to deny all trade and commerce by Confederates, including civilians.

Having proclaimed a blockade of the Confederate coastline from Virginia to Texas, the U.S. Navy had the daunting task of finding or building a sufficient number of ships to enforce this embargo along some 3,500 miles of hostile shores. Within days of the imposition of the blockade, the Union navy began purchasing existing ships of every description—from fishing schooners and ferryboats to steamboats and large yachts—and placed them into service. By the end of 1861, the navy had grown to more than 200 vessels, or approximately one ship for every 20 miles of coast. By concentrating the majority of their ships in front of or in close proximity to major harbors and usable transportation links to the interior of the Confederacy, authorities were able to curtail the influx of outside shipping considerably. Although effective, the high profits to be made by

*The blockader,* R.R. Cuyler, *was one of the many and varied ships used to enforce the Union blockade. (Peabody Museum, Salem, Massachusetts.)*

*A Confederate blockade-runner desperately flees a Union ship.*

blockade-runners and the lack of instant communications or technology constantly enticed sea captains to make the journey, and throughout the war, intrepid skippers brought their vessels safely into forbidden harbors.

Florida, as a part of the Confederacy at war with the Union, presented challenges and difficulties for both sides of the conflict. Florida, with its capacity to supply critical beef and salt to Confederate armies, was an essential part of the Southern war effort. Yet its sheer size and its some 1,400 miles of coastline made protecting and invading the state equally difficult, and, as a result, both Union and Confederate national governments devoted few resources to control the peninsula. The fact that the bulk of the state's population resided in a few counties in the interior of the peninsula compounded the problems of control or conquest even further. The absence of large urban areas, major railroad routes, or well-developed roads added to the difficulties of both attacker and defender.

Despite the scarcity of Union naval vessels to enforce the blockade in the first two years of the war, the judicious use of available ships, in combination with ground troops, made the policy effective. Very early on Confederate authorities conceded control of the major ports of Florida to Union forces. As events accelerated in Virginia and along the Mississippi, Union troops occupied Pensacola, Fernandina, St. Augustine, and present-day Jacksonville. Key West, although technically part of the peninsula, remained in Union

*This 1861 lithograph shows Fernandina as viewed from the St. Mary's River.*

*St. Augustine appears here during the Civil War. (U.S. Army Historical Institute, Carlisle Barracks.)*

*Jacksonville's waterfront is depicted in the 1860s. (Contemporary lithograph.)*

*This is a street scene in Key West in the 1860s. (Tebeau–Field Library of Florida History.)*

hands for the entire period of the war. So, too, did Fort Jefferson in the Dry Tortugas. At various times, Charlotte Harbor, Fort Myers, and Cedar Key were also occupied. These ports were islands of settlement surrounded by vast areas of virtually unoccupied and empty land. Captured with little difficulty and garrisoned by small detachments, the occupation of these centers did little to alter the military balance in the state. The most heavily populated areas remained firmly in the hands of Confederates, while the Union forces were restricted to smaller outposts.

The difficulties Florida presented to Confederate and Union strategists also provided golden opportunities for private individuals who soon took advantage of the state's extended coastline to erect salt works and to smuggle war materiel and consumer goods into the state. Although the principal harbors were occupied by Federal troops, the state had many small rivers and inlets that were capable of handling the flow of such goods into Florida and the shipment of tobacco, cotton, and naval stores out of the peninsula. As quickly as the Federal government established its blockade, determined individuals decided to ignore it. Many of these "blockade-runners" were Europeans, who saw a tremendous profit to be made in supplying civilian and military goods to the South and in supplying Southern agricultural products, particularly cotton, to eager European textile manufacturers.

Because most of Florida's rivers and bays were extremely shallow, the majority of the ships that attempted to run the blockade were shallow draft vessels, which could be sailed close to shore or steered into the narrow rivers and bays. This meant that their cargoes, entering or leaving, were usually very small. Instead of the hundreds of bales of cotton carried by pre-war ships, blockade-runners leaving Florida seldom carried more that three to five bales or more than ten barrels of turpentine or tobacco. The amount of goods brought into the peninsula by the same runners was also very small. For many Floridians, however, any successful out-voyage of agricultural products meant cash in the bank, while a successful in-voyage brought textiles and manufactured goods that otherwise would not be available.

To enforce the blockade, the Union navy created two separate squadrons initially, but soon divided their ships into four squadrons. The South Atlantic Blockading Squadron was given responsibility for the Confederate coastline from South Carolina to Key West and Cape Florida. Very quickly, ships were placed on station outside the major ports as far south as Jacksonville. The remainder of the east coast of Florida was policed by roving patrols that constantly moved up and down the coast.

Navigating the east coast was hazardous. Most of the operators of the lighthouses along this largely uninhabited stretch of land were Confederate sympathizers or were intimidated by locals who supported the Confederacy, so that by the end of the summer of 1861, none of these navigational aids were operational. The darkened coast was also thinly populated. The 1860 Census revealed that fewer than 200 families occupied the long stretch between Titusville and present-day Miami. The Indian River Lagoon, protected from the ocean by narrow barrier islands and with an average depth of 3 to 4 feet, offered blockade-runners access to Florida's interior via the St. Johns River, which was only 10 or so miles away. This north-flowing river provided a backdoor to the more heavily populated center of the state.

*The Indian River Lagoon offered shelter to small blockade-runners because of its broad expanse, shallow water, and isolated nature. (Tebeau-Field Library of Florida History.)*

Because of its shallow depth, the Indian River Lagoon provided a safe haven for blockade-runners using small sailing vessels with a centerboard that could be raised when negotiating the lagoon. Local fishermen and settlers knew the coastline intimately, and the absence of navigational lights presented few challenges. The close proximity of the Bahamas, Bermuda, and Cuba, with their open access to the manufacturers of Europe, proved to be an enticement that many smalltime entrepreneurs could not ignore. The lure of quick profits, combined with Confederate nationalism and a yen for adventure, made blockade running appealing.

The Indian River Lagoon had its drawbacks as a haven for runners. Despite its 150-mile length, there were only two inlets into the lagoon. The northern inlet, the Haulover Canal, was narrow and extremely shallow with an average depth of only 1 to 3 feet. Boats trying to enter the lagoon there were frequently dragged through the inlet into deeper water—usually after the cargo had been offloaded on the banks. This was a labor-intensive and time-consuming effort that invited the attention of the U.S. naval ships that patrolled this area on a frequent basis. As a result, runners seldom used the Haulover Canal.

The southern inlet at Jupiter provided an easier and quicker access to the lagoon. Wider and deeper, Jupiter Inlet presented fewer navigational hazards. It was also closer to the

Bahamas, which considerably shortened the open-ocean exposure for blockade-runners. The U.S. Navy, fully aware of this inlet, also regularly patrolled the mouth of the inlet. Even if a runner was able to avoid capture at sea, the narrow barrier islands, with their low foliage and mostly flat terrain, allowed U.S. naval vessels to observe activity in the lagoon from the ocean. Frequently, long boats manned by sailors and marines were sent into the lagoon to ambush or chase the runners. These forays were sometimes successful. In March 1863, for example, the commander of the *Beauregard*, acting in concert with the Federal schooner *Norfolk Packet* pursued the British schooner *Linda* up the Indian River Inlet. Although Union forces were forced to take to the shore when their boat was grounded, the *Linda* lowered its sails and surrendered after shots were fired. The British vessel was destined for New Smyrna with a cargo of salt, liquors, coffee, and dry goods.

Because of the absence of direct transportation routes into the interior, blockade-runners who were successful in evading the cordon of U.S. ships often had to store their goods on shore while arrangements were made to take them inland. U.S. naval commanders sent crews ashore to scout the shores of the inlet for camps and hidden caches of contraband. These raiding parties were occasionally successful.

The coastline north of the Indian River Lagoon was more heavily populated. The Mosquito Lagoon, which served as the primary port for the plantations that stretched

*Jupiter Lighthouse is located at the south end of the Indian River Lagoon.*

from New Smyrna to the St. Johns River and beyond, was deep enough to accommodate ocean-going steamships and sloops. Throughout the war, New Smyrna continued to attract blockade-runners, particularly those financed by British textile manufactures, who enjoyed some degree of success against the blockaders.

The activity in the Mosquito Inlet area continued to be a thorn in the side of the East Coast Blockading Squadron's commanders, and they were never able to close this port entirely. In March 1862, the Federal gunboats *Penguin* and *Henry Andrews* attempted to land forces at New Smyrna. Units of the Third Florida Infantry regiment refused to allow them to land. The commanders of the two ships were killed, along with three enlisted men, while the Confederate forces suffered no losses.

On March 2, 1863, the Federal gunboat *Sagamore* attempted to capture the Confederate blockade-runner *Florence Nightingale* as it was loading a cargo of cotton in Mosquito Inlet near New Smyrna. The *Sagamore* shelled the area from its position at sea and then sent men on barges to capture the ship. The captain of the *Nightingale* set fire to the ship to prevent its capture. Confederate forces on land repelled the Federal boarding crews. The fires on the blockade-runner were then extinguished, and the *Nightingale* successfully put to sea despite having lost its main mast and most of its provisions.

Four months later, a larger force, under the command of Lieutenant Commander English, was sent to deal with the problem of New Smyrna. On July 28, the USS *Beauregard* and *Oleander*, accompanied by the USS *Sagamore* and *Para*, launched an attack. After shelling the town, the Union forces destroyed several vessels tied up at the docks, including a sloop loaded with cotton, and burned large quantities of cotton on shore. Marines destroyed all buildings that had been occupied by Confederate troops. Despite this action, the port was reopened and continued to operate as a base for blockade-runners. On January 28, 1864, the U.S. schooner *Beauregard* reported the capture of the British blockade-runner *Racer* about 10 miles north of Cape Canaveral. The English vessel had just left New Smyrna bound for Nassau with a cargo of cotton. New Smyrna and Mosquito Inlet continued to demand attention from the U.S. Navy throughout the war.

The Blockading Squadron along the east coast of Florida became involved in other tasks. In addition to its duties against blockade-runners, the squadron also sent armed parties ashore to destroy salt works along the coast. Salt, a critical necessity for the Confederate civilian population and military establishment, was easily manufactured by the collection and distillation of seawater. Although the majority of Confederate salt works were located along the coast of the Gulf of Mexico, the simplicity of the manufacturing process and the high profits to be made ensured that hundreds, if not thousands, of individuals would try their hand at this venture. Because salt was an essential commodity, the squadron made every effort to destroy salt works wherever they found them. On March 22, 1862, two Federal gunboats, the *Penguin* and the *Henry Andrews*, operating in the area around New Smyrna, attacked Confederate salt works near Mosquito Inlet the day before they attacked the town. Such efforts often produced the most minimal results since the workers usually fled into the surrounding forests and the iron boilers and vats were difficult to destroy. After a few days wait, the works would be operational again.

Another task undertaken by the East Coast Blockading Squadron was to seek out and encourage Florida Unionists along the coast. In addition, the squadron undertook the task

*A Confederate torpedo was found in the St. Johns River in May 1864.*

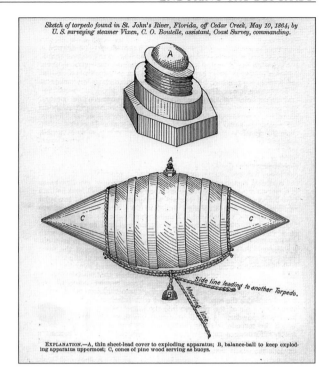

Sketch of torpedo found in St. John's River, Florida, off Cedar Creek, May 10, 1864, by U. S. surveying steamer Vixen, C. O. Boutelle, assistant, Coast Survey, commanding.

Side line leading to another Torpedo.

Mooring line

EXPLANATION.—A, thin sheet-lead cover to exploding apparatus; B, balance-ball to keep exploding apparatus uppermost; C, cones of pine wood serving as buoys.

of taking charge of runaway slaves and encouraging more to desert their masters. The sparse population of the east coast and the occupation of the key towns of Fernandina, Jacksonville, St. Augustine, and Key West by the Federal military made this a minor part of the squadron's activities.

Finally, the East Coast Blockading Squadron played an important role in the transportation of Federal army troops in their campaigns long the St. Johns River. In addition to transporting men and materiel, the squadron used its heavy guns against Confederate positions on the riverbanks and provided artillery support to Federal units occupying towns along the river.

Jacksonville, which commanded the entrance of the St. Johns River, was occupied by Federal troops four times during the war. The covering protection provided by the guns of the U.S. Navy allowed the army to hold this position and to use it as a base for Federal forays into the heavily populated areas of north and central Florida. The presence of Confederate "torpedoes," or mines, made the St. Johns dangerous for any Federal ship. On April 1, 1864, the *Maple Leaf*, a troop transport and supply ship, struck a Confederate torpedo on the St. Johns River and sank immediately in 3 fathoms of water. A detachment of Confederate artillery and a company of infantry troops were dispatched to the area to ensure that the wreckage was complete. Although life aboard a blockader could be tedious and boring at times, the element of danger was always present regardless of what mundane task was ordered.

On February 20, 1864, Union forces had received a major thrashing at Olustee and had retreated to Jacksonville. In May, Federal troops were sent up the St. Johns River toward Palatka, accompanied by a flotilla of gunboats, to attack the heart of the state's plantation belt. Although Union troops had previously occupied Palatka, they had been withdrawn following the defeat at Olustee. A Federal presence in the town, guarded by heavily armed gunboats, would give the Union forces control of this major waterway. As the gunboats *Ottawa* and *Columbine* provided protection, other ships began disembarking troops. Since the landing was unopposed, the *Columbine* left the *Ottawa* and moved south on the river.

Confederate troops, under the command of Captain J.J. Dickison, watched as the Union troops disembarked. Leaving most of his command in the breastworks at Palatka, he took a small force and two artillery pieces and pursued the *Columbine* up the river, hoping to intercept it at Brown's Landing, some 3 miles from the town. Although the *Columbine* moved cautiously, Dickison was not able to intercept it and he ordered a return to the entrenchments at Palatka. On his way back, he was met by a courier who informed him that the *Ottawa* and a troop transport were also moving south. Hurrying once again to Brown's Landing, Dickison waited for the arrival of the boats. At dusk, the *Ottawa* and its consort arrived and dropped anchor a short distance from the landing. As the Confederates prepared to fire at the boats, the sailors lit their lanterns, which made them easy targets for the Dickison's cannons. In the ensuing artillery duel, the Confederates drove off the troop transport and severely damaged the *Ottawa* before being driven off by the boat's 13 guns. The *Ottawa*'s crew was unable to get the boat moving until repairs were made, which took some 30 hours.

*Captain J.J. Dickison, seen here in a post-war photograph, fought constantly against Federal forces in East Florida and along the St. Johns River. (Tebeau-Field Library of Florida History.)*

The damage done to the *Ottawa* meant that the *Columbine*, which had gone ahead the day before, was now vulnerable to attack. Although not as heavily armed as the *Ottawa*, the boat did have several heavy artillery pieces on board and carried a crew of 148 sailors and infantry. The next day, Dickison led a detachment of sharpshooters and a battery of artillery pieces to intercept the *Columbine* before it could rejoin the *Ottawa*. Awaiting the boat's arrival at Horse Landing, Dickison was able to completely surprise the *Columbine*, and in a brief, 45-minute artillery attack, forced the vessel to surrender. Only 66 men of the boat's crew were alive and more than one-third of those were wounded. The Confederates suffered no casualties. After accepting the surrender of the *Columbine*, Dickison ordered the vessel burned to keep her from being retaken by several other Union gunboats that were coming to her rescue.

Despite the capture and destruction of the *Columbine* and the damage inflicted on the *Ottawa*, Dickison was not able to defeat the Union army along the river. The St. Johns campaign of 1864 was part of a larger Union plan to subjugate Northern and Central Florida, much as Sherman was doing in Georgia. In order for the Federal effort to succeed, the army would have to rely on the support and protection of the South Atlantic Blockading Squadron.

Along the Gulf Coast, the U.S. Navy was playing an even more important role. Patrolling the west coast of Florida was the responsibility of the East Gulf Blockading Squadron, which operated from Cape Florida to a point just east of Pensacola. This extended shoreline included the desolate and largely unpopulated region south of Tampa Bay as well as the more heavily settled areas along the Big Bend. Indeed, Florida's largest pre-war ports, Apalachicola and St. Marks, were located in the northern quadrant of the squadron's patrol area. So, too, was Cedar Key, the western terminus of the newly constructed railroad that ran across the entire peninsula to Fernandina. The myriad of small keys and deep ports offered greater opportunities for blockade-runners to find shelter. Many of the rivers that emptied into the Gulf of Mexico had their origins in Alabama and Georgia and, thus, offered potential invasion routes into the heart of the Deep South.

The Big Bend area was also in close proximity to the largest plantation areas of the state, as well as the areas of greatest production of naval stores. The existence of these industries, all of which were labor intensive, necessarily dictated that this area would also be home to the majority of the state's population, white and black, rich and poor. The pre-war antagonism between the dominant planter class and non-slaveholding whites meant the region also harbored the greatest number of opponents to the war. Many of these were members of the yeoman class who viewed the conflict as "a rich man's war, but a poor man's fight!"

Tallahassee, the state's capital, was situated just 40 miles or so from St. Marks, making it a tempting target for Union soldiers attached to the Blockading Squadron. Finally, the presence of large Union forces in Pensacola and Mobile, although in the operational sphere of the West Gulf Blockading Squadron, offered still more opportunities for possible major military action. Despite the many possibilities for direct involvement in a major military campaign, the East Gulf Blockading Squadron spent the entire war without doing so.

*The USS* Isonomia, *off the coast of Apalachicola, was typical of the coastal gunboats that enforced the blockade. (Mariner's Museum, Newport News, Virginia.)*

By May 1863, the East Gulf Squadron had 30 ships of various sizes in operation along the west coast of Florida. Nine ships were steam powered, heavily armed, and served as the main striking force of the squadron. A number of schooners, sloops, and barks were used as tenders for the larger ships or placed on patrol along stretches of the coastline where activity by runners was at a minimum. On March 15, 1865, C.K. Stribling, the commander of the squadron, reported a total of 38 ships on duty, armed with a total of 161 heavy guns. Although the number of ships assigned to the squadron had grown by almost a third, the number of steamers remained the same.

The steam-powered ships were necessary to chase and capture the larger sea-going vessels that bridged the blockade on an almost daily basis. A review of the reports of individual ship commanders in the *Official Records of the Union and Confederate Navies* reveals that open-sea chases of four to ten hours were common and that steamers provided the best means of catching blockade-runners that frequently were as technologically advanced as the ships of the squadron. Indeed, European-based runners often used ships that carried several masts in addition to side-wheels. Even the runners that were not steam powered were often fast sailing vessels that proved troublesome for even the steamers that chased them.

The cargoes carried by blockade-runners operating in the Gulf differed somewhat from those that worked Florida's eastern coast. Because the ships involved were frequently larger, the quantities carried in outbound bottoms were generally larger. The more developed transportation routes in the Big Bend region allowed for the collection and storage of greater quantities of cotton, timber products, and tobacco in warehouses for loading on outbound runners. For arriving cargoes, the same network of routes allowed for the transportation of heavy war materiel, such as lead, iron, and weapons to Tallahassee for shipment to armories and manufacturing centers. The same held true for the distribution of civilian goods, such as coffee, whiskey, textiles, and incidentals that made up the bulk of most inbound cargoes and that brought the highest prices and largest profits. Both the Confederate government and the government of Florida recognized the need for blockade-runners to make enough profit to justify the hazards of confronting the U.S. Navy and to underwrite the potential losses of ships, and both governments promulgated rules that mandated only about one-third of all incoming cargoes be strictly war materiel.

The East Gulf Blockading Squadron performed many of the same tasks as the South Atlantic Squadron—chasing runners, destroying salt works, supporting land campaigns by the U.S. Army—but its activities differed in two significant ways from those of the South Atlantic Squadron. One, the East Gulf Squadron occasionally undertook offensive operations on land, carrying out attacks on St. Marks, Cedar Key, Tampa, and Apalachicola. Most of these excursions achieved little in the way of a permanent or significant presence of Union troops, but they were bothersome and caused Confederate authorities to shift its forces to deal with them.

The greatest impact of the raids was that they allowed Union troops to make contact with the growing number of homegrown Unionists and deserters who populated the areas along the coast. As the Confederate military struggled against numerically superior forces in Virginia, along the Mississippi, and in Tennessee, the Confederate War Department demanded more and more troops from the Southern states. In April 1862, the Confederate Congress, seeking to bolster the number of reinforcements for its army, passed a Conscription Act that made all Southern men between the ages of 18 and 45 liable for service in the national army. State legislatures responded with similar laws that

*United States naval vessels blockade Tampa Bay in 1864. (Contemporary print.)*

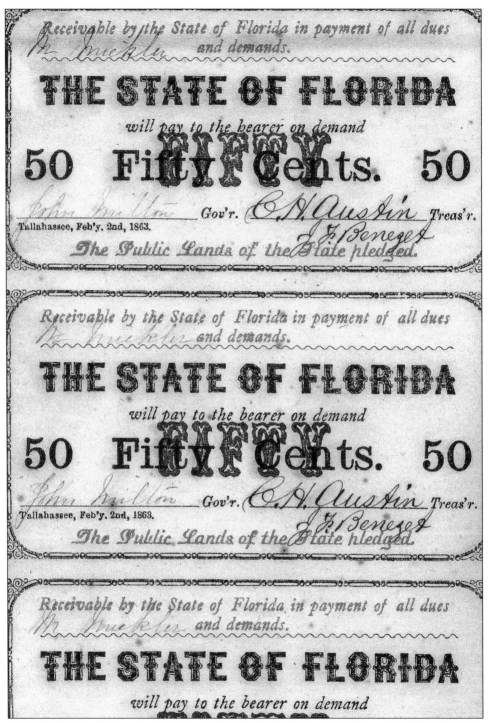

*Florida, other Southern states, and the Confederate government printed millions of dollars in paper currency during the war. The currency kept falling in value as the fortunes of the Confederacy declined. (Tebeau-Field Library of Florida History.)*

made service in state armies or militia units mandatory as well. Because the national and state conscription acts included a number of exemptions that could be used by persons of wealth and privilege, some Southerners, particularly men in the yeoman class, viewed these exemptions as further evidence that the war was being fought in the interests of the wealthy and sought to avoid the draft.

On April 24, 1863, the Confederate Congress levied a "tax-in-kind," which gave the Confederate government the right to collect one-tenth of all produce produced on farms and plantations during a calendar year. This tax, which was a logical answer to the cash-poor Confederate government's desperate need to pay for the war, was particularly onerous to the lower classes who frequently managed to "barely scrape by" each year on the foodstuffs produced on marginal farms. For many Southern families, the loss of husbands and sons to conscription had further reduced the crops and farm animals available for familial sustenance. Given the always-accelerating hyperinflation that made Confederate money virtually worthless, even those families that had hard cash seldom had enough to purchase sufficient replacement supplies.

There were those who, having volunteered for or been drafted into the Confederate military, decided that they no longer desired to be soldiers. Many of these simply packed their haversacks and made their way back home. Because the penalties for desertion were draconian—severe corporal punishment at the least or death at the worst—individuals who had "gone over the hill" were forced to be constantly on guard against Confederate authorities sent to arrest them. Often deserters banded together in small groups and lived in desolate areas that provided protection against recapture, often operating as bandit gangs that preyed on the surrounding farms and plantations. Individuals who simply saw an opportunity to engage in criminal activities often bolstered their numbers.

There were some staunch Unionists, who possessed an unyielding loyalty to the United States and who were frequently the target of harassment and violence from their Confederate neighbors. Largely unprotected by Confederate authorities, such people lived a haphazard existence, fraught with the possibility that they could lose their lives and property at any time.

The coast of the Gulf of Mexico was close to the largest slaveholding counties in Florida. As the demands for more soldiers depleted the number of white men in the army and as sporadic invasions and raids into the Florida peninsula drained the number of military units available to patrol the plantation region, a growing number of slaves took advantage of the situation to flee their masters. With little more than the stars to guide them, they made their way west to the coast. Along the way, they sometimes found refuge with Unionist families or joined the gangs of deserters operating in the swamps and forests.

Individuals and groups such as these, seeking the additional protection of the ships of the squadron, frequently sought out Union troops who came ashore. They provided valuable information about Confederate military activities, frequently served as pilots for naval vessels operating in coastal waters, and occasionally served as guides for raiding parties. In some cases, naval commanders supplied the gangs with arms, ammunition, and foodstuffs to encourage them to continue their disruptive activities, and enlisted runaway slaves in their crews.

Larger groups of Unionist individuals and families, who were not engaged in open opposition to the Confederacy, also sought out the ships of the squadron. Sensing an opportunity to embarrass Confederate authorities and to conduct an early form of psychological warfare, commanders established refugee centers at Fort Myers in southwest Florida, at Useppa Island in Charlotte Harbor, at Egmont Key in Tampa Bay, at Sea Horse Key and Cedar Key in the Big Bend region, at Hurricane Island in St. Andrew Bay, and at St. Vincent Island near St. Marks. On the east coast, the South Atlantic Blockading Squadron established a single camp at Mayport, at the mouth of the St. Johns River. These camps served as beacons for those seeking to escape Confederate rule.

The refugee camps also served as a source of recruits for the "Florida Rangers," a Union formation charged with conducting a guerrilla campaign against the Confederate irregulars who collected cattle for shipment north to Confederate armies. The idea for the Rangers came from Enoch Daniels, a veteran of the Third Seminole Indian War and a staunch Unionist. Daniels, who had joined the refugees on Useppa Island, took his idea to naval authorities, who sent him to squadron headquarters in Key West. There, General Daniel P. Woodbury, the army commander, and Rear Admiral Theodorus Bailey, the squadron commander, approved the idea and commissioned Daniels a captain and instructed him to go back to Useppa and raise his troop.

The Florida Rangers were an instant success. Over the next three months, the unit recruited from all of the refugee camps along the Gulf coast reached alliances with the various gangs of deserters operating near the coast and began a vigorous campaign of raids and reconnaissance against cattlemen rounding up beeves for shipment. Soon designated the U.S. Second Florida Cavalry, the unit's effective disruption of Confederate cattle operations soon led to the creation of the First Battalion Florida Special Cavalry, an irregular militia group commanded by Charles J. Munnerlyn, in March 1864.

Munnerlyn's cavalry had the primary duty of guarding both cowboys and cattle against the roving bands of deserters, Union sympathizers, and especially the Second Cavalry. Later on, the so-called "Cow Cavalry" was formally incorporated into the Confederate military and participated in a number of skirmishes along the Gulf coast.

George Buker, the noted historian of the blockading squadrons, argues that the non-naval activities of the East Gulf Blockading Squadron were its greatest achievement. Despite the capture of 283 blockade-runners during its four-year existence, which effectively closed the Gulf coast, Buker argues that the use of dissident groups to disrupt and damage the war effort on the Florida peninsula was much more important to the Union war effort.

The Union decision to blockade the coast of the Confederacy was a bold and audacious one. Ignoring the outcries of European nations and the restrictions of international law, the United States government established new laws and put national self-preservation above the niceties of convention. Like the many changes that occurred in the way armies fought and the use of new technologies to fight, the naval blockade marked a watershed in the ways in which wars were fought. Not only did naval ships manage to effectively deny the Confederacy the use of its 3,500 miles of coastline, the arming and equipping of anti-Confederate sympathizers presaged similar operations in other wars—World War II resistance movements, Vietnamese ethnic groups, and African tribal factions.

*This is a typical slave cabin in the plantation region of Florida.*

*These slave cabins are located on the Kingsley plantation near Jacksonville. Many former slaves continued to occupy these buildings long after the Civil War had ended. (Florida State Archives.)*

*Contrabands gather in front of the Provost Marshal's headquarters for this portrait in Jacksonville, c. 1864. (National Archives.)*

For Confederate Florida, the military operations conducted with the assistance and protection of the South Atlantic Blockading Squadron presented a constant threat to the state. So, too, did the presence of the East Gulf Blockading Squadron, and although this squadron did not participate in any major land campaigns, its effective blockade prevented the importation of critical civilian and military cargoes, as well as the export of cash crops that could be converted into credit for the Confederacy. By organizing and supporting the refugee population of the Gulf coast, the squadron was a disruptive force for Confederate authorities that made them allocate scarce resources to defend the peninsula.

# 7. Florida's War on the Home Front

Wars, by their violent nature, tend to disrupt entire societies in a myriad of ways. Few participants in the Civil War imagined the convulsions their worlds would face as a result of hostilities. This was certainly true in general for the South and for Florida in particular. The state's frontier level of development made it a prime candidate for the upheavals generated by the war and few areas remained untouched in some way. Every sector of Florida's diverse population felt war's hard fist and each responded as well as it could. While many were anguished and bitter by the Confederacy's ultimate defeat, a majority of Floridians was glad the turmoil and privation of four long years had come to an end.

Probably the first to experience the changes wrought by the Civil War were the 37,000 women in Florida. They watched as fathers, sons, brothers, and husbands packed up to join the rebel army. Florida regiments marched under flags women sewed and wore socks darned by their hands. Many women probably yearned to accompany their men to the fronts, while others no doubt chafed at not being consulted before male kin enlisted and shoved their daily responsibilities onto female shoulders. Women from all parts of the state faced the daunting task of maintaining businesses, farms, and families without much male support and guidance. For them, the war was an arduous event to be endured with little adventure or glory.

Women of Florida's planter class suffered the least and enjoyed the labor and company of their slave workforce. However, as the war progressed this relationship grew strained on a few plantations and especially on those without the services of a male overseer. Females cast in unfamiliar roles of farm manager, supply controller, and at times, disciplinarian, struggled to make do. Gentle ladies now gave orders to male slaves, almost unheard of before 1861, and hoped that their "people" would obey as they had in the past. Daily decisions about crop plantings, buying and selling of animals, and where to find needed items like cloth or medicine now weighed on them as never before. Only an occasional letter from a loved one offered advice, and such help was always welcomed.

The years of struggle leaned even heavier on yeoman class women living on small isolated farms. Without the aid of slave labor they had to be both father and mother to

*Southern women quickly adopted a "make do" attitude and coped with the shortages created by the war. (The Bettmann Archive.)*

their children, as well as chief provider for their families. Many relied on a network of relations and neighbors that modern single mothers could well appreciate. As darkness fell on their wilderness homes they fought back the fear that welled up inside them and hid it from their small ones. In the main they went on with the business of living under increasingly difficult circumstances. Their trials added to their confidence, and more than a few returning soldiers found wives less likely to defer to his judgment on family issues.

Shortages soon complicated the lives of all Floridians regardless of gender or class. Real coffee, tea, salt, and other once common products disappeared from store shelves or sold for inflated prices. Women were forced to seek substitutes from local plant life and rely on old folkways. Ancient spinning wheels and looms came out of storage and went back into service in an effort to provide the material needed for clothing. But the spiraling prices of food hurt women's effort to keep their families intact. By the end of 1862 the Florida state legislature acted to keep the kin of soldiers from starving or being reduced to wearing rags. The state government issued food to the hungry and items like cotton cards to make fabric, but such efforts never kept up with need. Soldier wives and children continued to suffer a declining standard of living, which did little to maintain the morale of Florida troops away at the fronts.

Luckless Florida women might have found themselves without even a roof over their heads during the Civil War. Union occupations of cities like Pensacola, Fernandina, Jacksonville, and St. Augustine forced many female-led families out of their dwellings and into the growing ranks of homeless refugees in the Confederate South as the war went on. Such refugees lived a hand-to-mouth existence and faced hard times almost daily. It was natural that women on the home front grew tired of these burdens and yearned for peace at any price. Some historians are convinced that the women's unwillingness to continue the struggle in 1865 even caused the general collapse of the rebel will to fight.

Florida saw a true civil war at home from 1861 to 1865, and Florida women were not immune from its cruelties. Unionists were harassed, beaten, and sometimes killed—leaving widows and orphans behind. Raiders from both Confederate and Federal camps attacked farms and plundered them without mercy to the women living there. On at least one occasion Florida women were taken into custody by the authorities and held hostage on account of their men's activities. This stood in sharp contrast to all the female work to support the war in the form of fund-raisers and drives to secure supplies for military hospitals. Southern ideals of the sanctity of womanhood indeed became a battlefield casualty of the war in Florida and elsewhere across the Confederate states.

At the same time, Confederate defeat or victory depended to a great degree on the tacit cooperation of the South's African-American slave population. Their labor on the farm, in factories, and in the government employ permitted the Confederacy to mobilize such a high percentage of its military-aged men for service. But as the war drifted toward becoming a struggle against the "peculiar institution," whites in Florida and other states wondered how long their bondservants would silently toil as chattel when freedom beckoned in the form of the Yankee army and navy. No slave revolts rocked the Florida peninsula during the war, but tensions between slave owner and slave increased as the war continued.

The bulk of Florida's roughly 62,000 slaves lived and worked in the counties of Middle Florida situated between the Apalachicola and Suwannee Rivers. The war touched this

*Runaway slaves, or "contrabands," made their way to Union outposts whenever they had the chance to do so safely. So many runaways flocked to Federal positions that some generals complained that they made it difficult to move their troops safely. (Library of Congress.)*

*Some runaway slaves joined the Union army. In Florida, many of the Federal units were made up of African Americans. (Library of Congress.)*

area very little compared with other areas of the state, though periodic Union raids raised the specter of mass escapes or bloody rebellion among slave owners. Neither of these ever occurred, but a steady stream of runaways slipped away from plantation and farm to the Federals east of the St. Johns River or to warships off the Gulf coast. Those making it to freedom often found work and the beginnings of a new life under Yankee protection. Those black slaves who remained soon heard of Lincoln's 1862 Emancipation Proclamation and felt that the day of liberation in Florida was just around the corner.

One of the provisions of the Emancipation Proclamation allowed for the enlisting of blacks into the Union military. Runaways from Florida in many cases went from being "contrabands" to being part of the almost 200,000 African Americans who served the North in the Civil War. These black Floridians, like their brothers from other states, proved their worth as combat troops. They also showed beyond a shadow of a doubt that they clearly deserved the freedom that they fought and died for on many fields of battle. Such veterans would return to Florida and play important roles in the state's post-war era.

The Confederacy, of course, was certain that their defeat would never come and depended heavily on slave labor in their war effort. Slaves could be found growing food for soldiers, working in salt plants and mills, and in cities. Southern military transportation needed them to drive wagons and haul supplies to the waiting armies. Others accompanied their masters into the army and did chores in army camps. Black Floridians carried out these duties for their owners or for the Confederate government directly.

Numerous examples of slave employment during the Civil War abound in Florida. Twenty slaves, held as prisoners in Madison County, were impressed to march down to

St. Marks to work fishnets there. Rebel authorities hoped that such seafood might help with the constant food shortages. Others found themselves leased directly to the Confederate War Department at the maximum fee of 25 Confederate dollars. They worked as teamsters moving government cargo around the state by wagon and even delivered cargoes of weapons without white escorts. Wartime records reveal that the rebel Quartermaster and Commissary Departments employed leased slaves in many of their Florida depots and warehouses.

Government-rented slaves also dug trenches and built fortifications at important points in the state, though at times their owners balked at having their "property" placed

*Despite some initial skepticism by whites in the North, black troops proved to be capable of holding their own in the heaviest of battles. (Library of Congress.)*

*Although African Americans provided much assistance to Confederate armies, the popular stereotypes of the "mindless and dangerous, but amusing" slave persisted among Southerners. (Contemporary lithograph.)*

anywhere near the dreaded Yankees. Crews of such laborers sweated as they removed extremely valuable railroad rails from unused tracks and hammered them down on the new line that ran across the state border into Georgia. At times slave workers got caught up in battle, or had the hard job of bringing home for burial a master, or a master's son, who had been killed in action. In the end the war brought freedom to all African-American Floridians regardless of their wartime experiences.

The war's fury also touched the native peoples of the Florida peninsula. Native Americans like the Seminoles had lived with and fought beside escaped African slaves for decades in the hammocks and swamps in the southern half of the state. When the Civil War came these Floridians had long experience with the horrors of war, having just barely survived the Second and Third Seminole Wars and their unpleasant consequences. Their numbers shrank due to casualties in these conflicts and forced deportations of tribal members to the trans-Mississippi region. One can only imagine what they thought upon learning the news that their old enemies were now killing each other in great numbers.

White Floridians, however, had strong opinions on the Seminoles and what they might do now that civil war was a fact. Many feared that the warriors might take advantage of wartime confusion and military weakness to once again tread the warpath and seek revenge for past defeats. Or even worse, these people might link up with their old allies, African slaves, and cause havoc up and down the peninsula. Rumors and a lack of real knowledge of the isolated Seminole bands' activities fueled speculation all over the Florida frontier. The Indians themselves had little desire to test their mettle against either Confederate Florida or the Union government, though Seminoles in far-off Oklahoma had established a relationship with the Confederate Bureau of Indian Affairs. South Florida Seminoles and Mikasuki tribes wanted nothing to do with the white man's war, but government officials could not dare to discount or ignore their presence.

The government in Tallahassee selected and dispatched a series of agents to travel to the south in search of the shadowy Seminole bands led by chiefs such as Sam Jones and Tiger Tail. Florida wanted to establish good relations with them and make certain that Seminole trade goods needs were met. Governor Milton even promised to meet with important leaders to cement a proper understanding between both parties. Such efforts took place in early 1862, just as Union forces were on the move and the new Confederate Conscription Act spurred draft evaders to take to the Florida woods. Friction with such persons might ignite a fourth Seminole war, a nightmare scenario that state leaders did not relish.

By the fall of that year panicked gossip of Seminoles preparing to attack remote settlers had most of South Florida worried. Due to the great excitement, Chief Sam Jones himself felt the need to set the record straight and sent a message to leading cattleman Jacob Summerlin. It told him that the tales of Seminole hostility were false, and asked that whites not launch a preemptive strike on his people. Summerlin believed the message and reported that violence was not imminent. Nothing happened, but both Seminoles and Floridians remained uneasy with each other until well past 1865.

The Seminole people did suffer during the Civil War, mostly due to major shortages of trade goods the tribe needed to live. Cloth for new clothing was always needed and soon in very short supply, as were the needles and thread necessary to manufacture such items. Probably the most important was the shrinking supply of gunpowder and lead for bullets required for their Kentucky hunting rifles. Traders who had once supplied the tribe vanished, and the natives despaired of securing what they needed. Without munitions, in particular, the Seminoles could not hunt for the meat they needed to sustain them, and might have to take the powder and shot from whites in order to survive. With this in mind, state agents went to immense lengths to deliver these to the tribal bands even in the middle of civil war. The complications of doing this paled in comparison to the causing of an Indian uprising that could very well cut off access to the large cattle herds grazing south of Lake Okeechobee.

Native Floridians did indeed have contacts with Union forces, which did little to calm Confederate fears. Seminoles met with woodcutting parties from Federal-occupied Key West along the banks of the Miami River and exchanged items. In May 1864 a small party of Mikasukis visited the Yankee base at Fort Myers. While there they denounced the Confederacy, expressed a desire to be the friends of the Union, and received presents from the garrison in return. The Mikasukis were pleased to see United States Colored troops stationed at Fort Myers. The sight of these warriors brought back memories of past biracial alliances between the two groups that helped hold off much of the U.S. Army during the Second Seminole War.

*Florida Seminoles maintained a neutral posture during the Civil War. (Florida State Archives.)*

In the end, Florida's Mikasukis and Seminoles maintained rough neutrality, stuck as they were between the North and the South during the Civil War, and may have been able to play both ends against the middle while trying to simply stay alive. While Seminoles in the west actually joined and fought with the Confederate army, there is no solid evidence that any member of the South Florida tribe ever did so. When the conflict ground to a halt these natives remained in their Everglades strongholds and had few contacts with whites for much of the rest of the 19th century. Their wartime experience consisted of want and disruption, as was the case with most residents of the Florida peninsula.

Not surprisingly, Florida's Hispanic population was drawn into the conflict from its early days. During two long periods as a Spanish colony the peninsula's Latin community laid down very deep roots and, in time, was augmented by immigrants from Cuba, Mexico, and Spain itself. Dr. Andrew Turnbull's ill-fated 1768 New Smyrna settlement introduced hundreds of Minorcans whose descendants remained in the St. Augustine area well in the 1860s. Significant numbers of ethnic Minorcans signed on with volunteer companies like the St. Augustine Blues, which later became Company B of the Third Florida Infantry Regiment. Soon every Florida Civil War military unit had at least one member with a Hispanic name on its muster role, and these soldiers often distinguished themselves on battlefields in the east and the west.

Others stepped forward to help defend Florida itself from continuing Yankee threats. Volunteer Coast Guard companies formed to help shield Tampa Bay's long, vulnerable coastline, and counted Hispanics among its members. One member of the Coast Guard recorded in his diary on February 23, 1862, that his was "a cosmopolitan company, it is composed of Yankees, Crackers, Conchs, Spaniards . . . but all are good Southern men." At least eight other men of Hispanic origin served as coastguardsmen during the early weeks of the war.

As was the case with Seminoles and African Americans, Floridians of Hispanic ancestry at times endured friction with the greater Anglo community in the state during the War

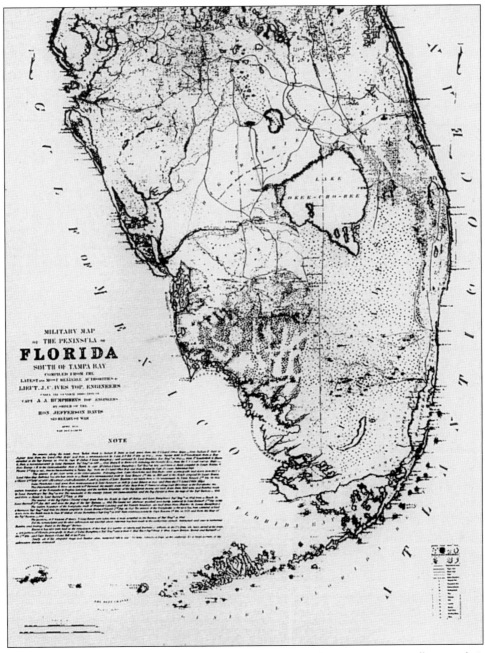

*The difficult terrain of South Florida and the isolated locations of Native American villages made it difficult for the Confederate authorities and traders to maintain contacts with the small Indian population of the state. (Tebeau-Field Library of Florida History.)*

between the States. The experience of Antonio A. Canova is a case in point. Canova was a well-known citizen of northeast Florida during the antebellum years. Though 36 years old, he enlisted in Company A of the Third Florida Infantry as a private in 1861. Not destined to shoulder a musket for long, Canova received a commission as a major in the Confederate Commissary Department in 1862. By December of that year he was selected to be Florida's chief of subsistence and charged with collecting and forwarding needed supplies to feed rebel soldiers and animals.

Major Canova soon had more than his share of detractors due to problems in adequately provisioning military units stationed in Florida. One officer in the Second Florida Cavalry angrily protested in a letter home in 1862 that his troopers went hungry as a result of poor commissary work and that "Major Canova wont get any votes in this section." In the same letter he charged that Canova was "like the rest of Manaucians [sic] when he gets power he feels he is of more importance that he should." Canova himself would soon be caught up in a legal dispute arising from his military duties that tested the powers of the Confederate government and the commitment of wartime Floridians to the cause.

In July 1863, ex-U.S. Senator David Levy Yulee negotiated a business deal wherein some 50 large hogsheads of valuable sugar would be sold to agents representing the city of Savannah, Georgia. But before delivery of the kegs, Major Canova learned of the arrangement and seized the sugar in the name of the Confederate States for military use.

*This monument dedicated to Confederate soldiers from St. Augustine was visited by Ulysses S. Grant during his trip to the city in 1879. Among the soldiers who served the Confederacy were men of Spanish and Minorcan descent.*

He based his authority to do so under the controversial Impressment Act. An outraged Yulee immediately brought suit in the Florida courts claiming that Canova had no such legal authority to impress sugar or any other foodstuffs for rebel use. As the Confederate States had not set up a national supreme court, the Florida state supreme took the case and made the decision in *Yulee v. Canova* (1864).

The justices sitting in Tallahassee agreed with Yulee and ruled in his favor and against Canova and the Confederate government. Even in the midst of civil war, state rights and property privileges remained paramount over the needs of the national government, as this Florida case clearly showed. Rebel authorities, again without any higher appellate court, reluctantly accepted the verdict and released the sugar. The legal proceedings were followed with considerable interest throughout the southern section of the Confederacy, making Antonio Canova probably Florida's best-known ethnic Hispanic in the Civil War, but far from the most popular.

With the end of the fighting in 1865, Florida's Hispanics could look back with some pride at the conduct of their sons and daughters in support of their state and the Southern cause. Their military experience both in and outside Florida encapsulated that of all the Civil War soldiers, while on the home front they shared the hardships and the heartaches of those times. They too longed for peace and the safe return of loved ones from the army. Though almost ignored by historians of the Florida's Civil War, Hispanic Floridians made noteworthy contributions to the struggle and acted in ways deserving of praise and remembrance.

While Civil War Florida saw divisions in terms of race, gender, and ethnicity, the greatest rip in the state's social fabric involved those citizens who supported the Confederacy and those who remained loyal to the Union. This schism came into being with secession and the firing on Fort Sumter and only grew worse and more bitter. Leaders such as Governor John Milton knew from the very start that not all Floridians supported the actions of 1861 and that the pressures of the conflict might drive more people into the loyalist camp. Initially members of this group tended to be individuals of Northern descent or with family or commercial ties to that region. Often antebellum political alignments paved the way to Unionism for Floridians. Concentrations of such people existed in many Florida cities and grew as they came under the protection of the Union army. Jacksonville, Fernandina, St. Augustine, and Key West all hosted a core of Unionist sentiment during the war years.

As the realities of wartime life became too clear to Floridians, many began drifting toward an allegiance with the old government. This is especially true among frontier families who could argue that the Confederates had seemingly done little for them but take their cattle and their sons away. Conscription and impressment drove many into the Union camp, and government efforts to enforce these laws increased tensions and often led to violence and reprisal. Raiding and counter-raiding among these groups created a climate of danger and fear in parts of Florida that would not fade until well past Reconstruction.

Florida Unionists had no sooner organized themselves than they sought to contact the Lincoln Administration for help and political patronage in the occupied areas. They asked for aid on issues like loyal slaveholders being able to hold on to their property or for permits to legally ship cotton, lumber, and turpentine northward through the blockade. Good Union men could expect to be rewarded in this fashion, and many accepted Federal appointments handed out by Washington. They hoped that this might lead to the re-creation of a loyal state government without the influence of old rivals. Men like Lyman D. Stickney and Harrison Reed (a future state governor) took leadership positions in the new order. Others, shadow Unionists like James McKay and Ossian B. Hart, walked a fine line between the two forces with the idea of reaping as many benefits of such neutrality as they could.

Unionists were encouraged in their work by Northern schemes to aid Florida's reconstruction by settling Yankee veterans or freed slave on the peninsula. The ultimate goal would be to get Florida cotton production flourishing and feed the hungry textile mills of New England. While none of these ideas ever got off the ground, they did show how interested the Federal government was in Unionism in Florida. However, that same government's military policies, like the occupation and then abandonment of Jacksonville, hurt loyalists trying to build a political base among the populace.

Florida Unionists peaked in their influence in 1864 as the Lincoln forces geared up for a tough, if not impossible, re-election campaign for the president. Desperate for electoral votes to keep their man in office, Republicans hoped that far-off Florida might provide some if it could be rehabilitated in time for the fall election. President Lincoln's "ten percent plan" offered a solution since if only ten percent of a state's 1860 registered voters

*Harrison Reed, who came to Jacksonville as a postal agent, was a prominent Republican who was elected governor of Florida during Reconstruction. (Florida State Archives.)*

would take an oath of allegiance that area could form a new state government and participate in national elections. Presidential secretary John Hay was dispatched to the peninsula to supervise the registration and fend off the attempts of Secretary of the Treasury Salmon P. Chase to derail Lincoln's re-nomination. Hay fell in love with the lush Florida landscape while on his mission and even bought a few parcels of land for his own future use. All his work produced few hard results, and the political operators soon learned that the bulk of Florida was still under rebel control and the quick reconstruction was but a dream. This point was hammered home in February 1864 with the thrashing of Federal troops at the battle of Olustee.

*Lyman D. Stickney was a supporter of Salmon P. Chase's bid for the Republican president nomination in 1864, but it did not prevent him from writing to Abraham Lincoln assuring him of his support for the president. (Abraham Lincoln Papers.)*

Across the length and breadth of Florida, Unionists and Confederates would wage their own relentless civil war that witnessed extreme violence on both sides. Men like Henry A. Crane, W.W. Strickland, and Enoch Daniels, among others, raised Union raiders from the local population with relative ease as the war went on. Armed and supplied by U.S. Navy blockaders and bases like those at Fort Myers and Cedar Key, these groups swept though Middle and South Florida and hampered rebel cattle-driving. Pro-Southern forces like the Cow Cavalry retaliated in kind and added to the bloodshed on Florida's home front.

In time regular Union military leaders concluded that such irregular forces needed the structure and discipline of being part of a formal command. In October 1863 the First Florida United States Cavalry regiment was organized at Fort Barrancas near Pensacola. It generally operated in the Panhandle region of West Florida and, in 1865, helped capture and occupy Mobile and Montgomery, Alabama. The regiment's war ended when it mustered out of Federal service on November 17, 1865. A sister unit, the Second Florida United States Cavalry regiment, came into existence at Key West and Cedar Key in late 1863. Many of its recruits were Unionist refugees and they soldiered in the Fort Myers–Tampa Bay area to 1865. In March of that year the Second Florida moved northward to participate in the ill-fated campaign to capture Tallahassee. When the guns finally grew quiet this regiment did occupation duty in Tampa until discharged on November 29, 1865.

During the summer of 1865 the commanding officer of the Second Florida had to warn his men that aggressive foraging and acts of vengeance against pro-Confederate Floridians were no longer permissible and would not be tolerated in his regiment. These soon to be ex-soldiers had to learn not only to live in peace with former enemies, but were now required to protect them and their property. This strange new world dawned for all the participants in Florida's Civil War on the home front. Women, free and enslaved African Americans, Seminoles, Hispanics, and Unionists now found themselves in a society being transformed, and few understood what the new social order would entail. Few could even imagine that in only 30 years their state would radically change and see the birth of modern Florida. However, for most minority Floridians the "new birth of freedom" promised by the Civil War would be delayed for generations.

# 8. A Not-So-United Florida
## Unionists

Although the Florida Secession Convention of 1861 had hastily carried Florida into the Confederate fold, there were those in the state who refused to support the new Southern nation. Collectively referred to as "Unionists," these individuals remained supporters of the Federal government for a variety of reasons, ranging from heartfelt and sincere political differences to more banal reasons such as avoiding the Confederate draft.

Richard Keith Call, an intimate of Andrew Jackson and former territorial governor, was adamant in his opposition to secession, referring to it as treason in a pamphlet he published on December 1, 1860. Call, along with a number of other prominent Floridians, had been the backbone of the Constitutional Unionist party that had opposed the ardently secessionist Democrats in state elections in October 1860. Edward Hopkins, who represented the Unionists, had polled 5,248 votes in the gubernatorial campaign that year but lost out to hard-line secessionist John Milton, who received 6,994. The 1860 elections demonstrated a significant opposition to the question of secession among Florida's 77,000 whites.

Throughout the presidential and state elections of 1860, individuals who expressed their opposition to secession were harassed by their opponents. Although prominent planters and politicians, such as Call and others, were only verbally harangued, lesser-known people were sometimes physically attacked and driven from the state. A small number were shot at, and at least one individual was reported as having been wounded. The property of strong Union men was also attacked, and those who were in business were sometimes subjected to boycotts by their customers. Life in Florida for a staunch Unionist was not a pleasant or comfortable existence.

Although feelings ran high in the electoral preludes to the Secession Convention in January 1861 and despite the fact that several members of the former Constitutional Unionist party who had been elected to the Convention tried to delay the final action of that body, Democrats were not to be denied. Secession moved from the stage of political theory and debate to reality. While the number of voters who were opposed to secession was significant, once secession had triumphed, the majority of Floridians threw their support to the new order.

The final decision to secede brought about some significant changes in the ranks of the opponents to secession. Some, like George T. Ward, Jackson Morton, and David S. Walker, were known as "Reluctant Confederates," who, having expressed their opposition to secession, nevertheless joined the Confederate cause in defense of their state, class, or neighbors. Their attempts to defuse the secessionist trend and to block the final vote in the Convention did little to diminish their political or social standing. Ward and Morton were delegates to the Provisional Congress of the newly formed Confederate States of America, while Walker continued to serve as a justice on the Florida Supreme Court. In 1866, Walker was elected governor, a position he held until mid-1868.

Some individuals who had actively opposed secession remained steadfast in their opposition to it. Ossian Bingley Hart, a lawyer and a former state representative from St. Lucie County, was the son of a slave owner and his social, economic, and political interests were closely aligned with those of members of the dominant planter class. Despite these similarities, Hart was unyielding in his opposition to secession. During the war, he suffered greatly as a result of his fierce beliefs. In 1873, he was ultimately rewarded for his wartime support of the Union when he was the successful Republican candidate for governor.

Many of the strongest Unionists in Florida were located in extreme East and West Florida; Escambia County (Pensacola) and Duval County (Jacksonville) sent a pro-Union delegation to the Convention. These were areas that had enjoyed dominance during the periods of Spanish and English control but that had lost importance with the emergence of the plantation economy following the purchase of Florida by the United States. These areas, which quickly fell under Union control at the beginning of the war, provided some refuge for Floridians who had to flee their homes to escape the wrath of their Confederate neighbors. Fernandina, Pensacola, St. Augustine, Jacksonville, and Key West offered sanctuary for persecuted Unionists, while temporary refugee camps created by the East Gulf Blockading Squadron at Fort Myers, Useppa Island, and other coastal areas in West Florida also provided safe havens. Individuals who fled to Union lines were likely to lose the property they left behind, since the Sequestration Act of 1861 allowed Confederate officials to confiscate and dispose of the property of "enemy aliens."

President Abraham Lincoln had enticed many of the more politically minded Unionists to seek refuge in Union-held areas when he announced his "ten-percent plan," by which a state might be restored to the Union if ten percent of the 1860 electorate would take an oath of allegiance to the United States and register to vote. To this end, he had dispatched his personal secretary, John Hay, to follow the Federal army into Florida to recruit voters for this purpose.

Despite the early occupation of some of Florida's coastal towns by the Federal military, life as a Unionist refugee was not without its risks. Although some towns, such as Key West and Fernandina, were never evacuated by Federal forces, others, such as Jacksonville, saw occupation forces come and go several times. Decisions by Federal commanders to move troops or to abandon certain points made security for Unionists an "iffy" proposition, and when Union troops left, they left too. Occasional attacks or raids by

The troops of the United States have come amongst you to protect loyal citizens and their property from further molestation by the creatures of a rebel and usurped authority; and to enable you to resuscitate a government which they have ruthlessly endeavored to destroy.

All loyal people who return to, or remain at their homes, in the quiet pursuit of their lawful avocations, shall be protected in all their rights, within the meaning and spirit of the Constitution of the United States. The sole desire and intention of the Government is, to maintain the integrity of the Constitution and the laws, and reclaim States which have revolted from their national allegiance, to their former prosperous and happy condition.

There is great satisfaction in the fact, now become patent to all, that a large portion of you still cling, in your hearts, to that Mother who first liberated you from the thraldom of a despotic government; who next rescued you from the deathly grasp of the wily savage, at a frightful cost of life and treasure; and who afterwards elevated you from the condition of territorial dependence to that of a proud and independent State.

I earnestly recommend that in every city, town and precinct, you assemble in your primary and sovereign capacity, that you there throw off that sham government which has been forced upon you, swear true fidelity and allegiance to the constitution of the United States, and organize your government and elect your officers in the good old way of the past.

When this is done, then will you see the return of prosperous and happy days, in the enjoyment of that trade and industry to which your ... coast is so well adapted, and in the immunity from that want and suffering to which you have been so wickedly subjected by the traitorous acts of a few ambitious and unprincipled men; then will you enjoy the fruits of your honest labor, the sweets of happy homes, and the consolation of living under those wise and salutary laws that are due only to an industrious and law-abiding people.

T. W. SHERMAN,
BRIGADIER-GENERAL, COMMANDING.

Head Quarters, Expeditionary Corps, }
Jacksonville, Fla., March 20, 1862. }

*Federal authorities assured Jacksonville residents that United States troops would ensure the safety of all loyalists. (Tebeau-Field Library of Florida History.)*

*This notation was made in the register of the Hodson House, Jacksonville's premier hotel, when Federal troops evacuated the city on April 8, 1862. According to the note, "about two hundred of our citizens left on [the] Cosmopolitan, going north." (Tebeau-Field Library of Florida History.)*

Confederate forces added to the sometimes-precarious existence of refugees. By and large, however, these towns offered as much protection for Unionists as could be found anywhere in the South.

Within the coastal towns controlled by Federal forces, certain individuals rose to prominence—individuals who would play important roles in post-war Florida. In Key West, William S. Marvin, who had first come to the city as a federal judge before statehood in 1845 and who had served in the legislature and constitutional convention, continued to serve in the judiciary. In East Florida, John Sammis, who had moved to Jacksonville before the war and who was married to a daughter of Zepheniah Kingsley, headed a group of Unionists who were supporters of Abraham Lincoln.

These pre-war Unionists were joined by a growing number of political opportunists who came to the area as part of the Federal occupation. These "scalawags" saw an opportunity to seize power and to elevate themselves to positions of importance. Some came as agents of rival factions in the Republican Party seeking control of the U.S. presidency. In October 1862, Salmon P. Chase, U.S. secretary of the treasury and a political rival of Lincoln, dispatched tax collectors to the occupied areas to lay the foundations for a "restored" Florida under Lincoln's ten percent plan that would be supportive of his presidential ambitions. Lyman D. Stickney and Harrison P. Reed headed up the pro-Chase movement in East Florida.

Attempts to enroll ten percent of the electorate were not successful. Although Federal forces controlled the coastal areas of the state, all attempts to conquer the more populated interior regions of Florida were unsuccessful. For both Lincoln and Chase, the resounding defeat of the Federal army at the Battle of Olustee in February 1864 spelled defeat for wartime efforts to restore Florida.

Although Florida had not been restored, a Republican Convention was held in Jacksonville in May 1864. Pro-Lincoln delegates dominated the convention, and those who had supported Chase found themselves left out in the cold. The Chase campaign to win the Republican nomination was rejected by the National Republican Convention, and Chase supporters in Florida quickly adjusted their allegiances to reflect the reality of the situation.

*Albert Sammis of Jacksonville was born a slave on a Florida plantation but rose to prominence in Republican politics. (University of North Florida Library.)*

*General Alexander S. Asboth was the Federal army commander in West Florida. He was wounded in the attack on Marianna in September 1864.*

The areas under Union control also attracted a significant number of runaway slaves. "Contrabands," as they initially were called, provided a wealth of military intelligence for Federal commanders, hurt the Confederate manufacturing and agricultural efforts, disrupted the local civilian population, and also provided recruits for the Union army and navy. Contrabands also provided Unionists, who became Republicans, with an opportunity to establish working relationships with them. When these former slaves were enfranchised after the war, they provided the base for the Republican Party in Florida and filled local and state political offices.

Unionists in West Florida were also able to flourish under the protection of the Federal army. Pensacola, which had been abandoned by Confederates on May 9, 1862, became the main collection point for Unionist refugees from southern Alabama, Georgia, and the Florida Panhandle. The umbrella of protection provided by General Alexander S. Asboth's troops and the ships of the West Gulf Blockading Squadron also attracted a growing number of Confederate deserters and draft dodgers.

The Florida Panhandle was a center of pro-Union activities. In the 1860 election for delegates to the Secession Convention, Escambia, Santa Rosa, and Walton Counties chose men who were pledged to the Union cause. In Jackson County, home of fire-eating governor-elect John Milton, Unionists made a strong showing, while Leon and Gadsden

Counties reported a strong anti-secessionist vote. Whether or not the returns reflected actual voting or, as some charged, control of the ballot box by Democrats, it can be safely asserted that a significant portion of the regional population remained loyal to the Union or became only half-hearted Confederates.

In Washington County, the sheriff, Abram M. Skipper, refused to serve under Confederate authorities, preferring instead to seek refuge with Union forces. Naval authorities of the East Gulf Blockading Squadron were in constant contact with Unionists along the Panhandle coast. Some of these were certainly opportunists who adopted the Union cause in order to further their own business interests, as was the case of four Marianna merchants who contacted the skipper of the USS *Reckless* with a proposal to allow them to flee through the blockade with 120 bales of cotton aboard their schooner. One of these men, John T. Myrick, was a merchant and a plantation owner with 97 slaves. His sons were in the Confederate army. Of course, the request was made in January 1864, a time when it appeared that Union armies from Pensacola and Jacksonville would sweep through North Florida and isolate the peninsula from the Confederacy.

Captain James McKay of Tampa was also a Unionist by opportunity. In mid-1861, he used his cattle steamer *Salvor* to carry supplies to Federal troops stationed in the Dry Tortugas and Key West. He even leased his ship to the U.S. Navy and retuned to Tampa. There Confederate authorities charged him with treason and forced him to post a $10,000 bond to ensure his loyalty. McKay was allowed to go back to Key West and reclaim his steamer. In October 1861, blockaders captured the *Salvor* carrying a cargo of pistols and percussion caps, and he was held in Key West. Soon sent to Washington, McKay was released on parole after he swore an oath of allegiance to the United States. In April 1862, he returned to Tampa and obtained a new steamer. From mid-1862 until October 1863, he was engaged in running the blockade. Apparently, McKay could be a Confederate or Unionist—depending on who had the money and the power.

Confederate Brigadier General Richard F. Floyd, worried about residents in the Apalachicola region who might assist the Union fleet, ordered the evacuation of that town in March 1862. Floyd placed several river pilots under arrest and had them shipped north to Chattahoochee. Governor John Milton made repeated requests to Confederate authorities to maintain a sizeable force of soldiers in the Panhandle, particularly near his hometown of Marianna, "because in the counties bordering the Gulf and especially Washington County, there are many deserters from other states." One Jackson County physician reported, "the county for fifty miles between here and the Gulf is infested with hundreds of deserters in communication with the enemy." Who could blame them, he asked, "They had not been paid since June and their families were suffering from want of food."

The large number of deserters and Unionists in the Panhandle and along the western coast provided Union authorities with a unique opportunity to create problems for Confederate authorities in Florida. In combination with the commander of the Union army at Key West, Asboth began to actively recruit troops from the ranks of refugees and deserters for service in the Union army. The formation of a new unit would greatly improve his ability to conduct offensive operations in the Panhandle. In December 1863, Asboth received approval for creating and mustering into service the First Florida Cavalry

*Prince, a runaway slave, was a river pilot for the USS* Uncas *and was typical of the "contrabands" who actively aided the Union cause in Florida. (Florida State Archives.)*

Regiment of U.S. Volunteers. By March 1864, the regiment was operational and in the field.

In the summer of 1864, Asboth's command began an active campaign in the Panhandle region. Between July 20 and 29, units of the Second U.S. Colored Infantry and the Second Florida U.S. Cavalry, also a unit made up of deserters and Unionists, attacked Confederate forces in and around St. Andrew Bay. On September 18, General Asboth led a force of about 700 men from Fort Pickens into the Panhandle. As he proceeded, he captured a number of small Confederate detachments and enlisted new recruits for his First Florida Cavalry. On September 26, Asboth defeated a small Confederate force at Campbellton. The next day, he captured Marianna. Wounded in the action, Asboth withdrew to Pensacola, taking with him some 400 slaves, 200 horses, and 400 head of cattle.

Despite his superior force, Asboth was not able to hold the territory he had captured. The North Florida area was the only area of the state that had a working railroad that could be used to shift Confederate forces in sufficient numbers to defeat him. Florida troops were rushing to head him off from any further incursion. The area's close proximity to Georgia, which had a large Home Guard and a much more expansive network of railroads, was too much of a threat to be ignored, and although that state was reeling under the onslaught of Sherman's March to the Sea, state troops were already being assembled to deal with this possible invasion.

*This cadet most likely came from the West Florida Seminary. (Historical Association of Southern Florida.)*

*Union reinforcements arrive at Fort Pickens. (*Leslie's Illustrated Newspaper.*)*

The campaign against Marianna was the last major offensive of 1864. In March 1865, a Union force landed near St. Marks for a campaign against Tallahassee. On March 6, a ragtag force of militia, recuperating wounded Confederate soldiers, and seminary cadets rebuffed this Federal attack at the Battle of Natural Bridge.

Although there would be no more major confrontations between the warring parties in West Florida, the region continued to be a bother for Confederate authorities until the end of the war a month later. The passions and conflicts over secession, the Confederacy, and the Civil War would continue for several years, however. During Reconstruction, this area became one of the bloodiest regions of the state as Democrats battled Republicans for control of state government and as whites battled blacks for economic, political, and social control.

# 9. Battles in Civil War Florida

The American Civil War was a titanic struggle waged by huge armies over almost half a continent. Large-scale battles tested the mettle, training, and discipline of the soldiers involved regardless of side. Obscure places became known for the fights they witnessed, and a few sites became immortal. But for the men on the firing lines battles were small things that existed only in their immediate vicinity. Strategies and generals meant little to troops on smoke-shrouded fields struggling to stay alive and do their duty. It really mattered little whether one was engaged at Gettysburg or in a small skirmish in an operational backwater. The bullets were the same and caused the same deaths and injuries with equal certainty. For the soldiers in blue and gray all battles were important as their lives were literally on the line in each one.

What of Civil War combat in the state of Florida? The peninsula could not boast of campaigns or fierce clashes on the scale of Shiloh or Antietam. Both Union and Confederate leaders assigned relatively few units to the region and, with few exceptions, were locked in a strategic stalemate. Neither side could or would commit the needed troops to decisively defeat the other and eject them from Florida. So Florida's war would consist of what the *Official Records* refer to as "affairs, actions, or skirmishes" and the like. Only on rare occasions would events worthy of full-blown battle status occur. But again for the men involved such incidents were vitally important and matters of life and death.

One such serious engagement took place early in the war on Santa Rosa Island near Pensacola. In October 1861, the uneasy peace in the area was shattered when a force of nearly 1,000 rebel soldiers, all volunteers, landed on the island with the intention of raiding the outlying defenses and camps near Fort Pickens. Defending these were the Sixth New York Infantry regiment and various other Federal troops. The Confederates, under the command of General Richard H. Anderson, splashed ashore on the night of October 9 and slogged through the sandy ridges toward the unsuspecting enemy. Their surprise was almost complete as Yankee pickets went running for cover and musket fire broke the still night air.

*The Battle of Santa Rosa Island is illustrated here, October 9, 1861. (*New York Illustrated News.*)*

*Confederate troops man a battery of columbiads at Pensacola in 1861. (National Archives.)*

The Sixth New York stumbled from their tents and fell back toward Pickens with some confusion. Their camp went up in flames after being ransacked by the Confederates eager for souvenirs. Soon however reinforcements from Fort Pickens arrived and added the weight of their numbers to the on-going firefight. The rebels soon realized that seizing any artillery batteries or spiking their guns was now out of the question and soon began their own retreat back to the boats and a return to the mainland. The cost of this attack for the Confederates was 18 killed, 39 wounded, and 30 taken prisoner. Union troops lost 14 killed, 29 wounded, and 20 lost as prisoners of war. Union commander Colonel Harvey Brown complimented his enemies across the bay by calling their raid "judicious" and potentially costly to Federal efforts around Pensacola. Both sides left Santa Rosa with a clear understanding of what war was about, especially the price paid in dead and wounded comrades. Soon there would be other lessons.

The spring of 1862 saw a shift in the military situation on the Florida peninsula. The Richmond government had made the hard decision to withdraw the bulk of their fighting forces from the state and use them in more vitally threatened locations. At the same time growing Union military strength allowed them to send soldiers and ships to strike at coastal Florida towns and make bases of them to support the naval blockade and for future land movements. Local Confederates were not able to mount much more than token resistance to such operations. Fernandina, Jacksonville, and St. Augustine began periods of permanent or temporary occupation. Defenders of the St. Johns River, an obvious

*Union occupation troops are pictured in St. Augustine. (Library of Congress.)*

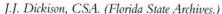

*J.J. Dickison, CSA. (Florida State Archives.)*      *Major General Quincy Adams Gilmore, USA.*

highway into the state's interior, met stinging defeat at Yellow and St. Johns Bluffs at the hand of aggressive Federals. Union troop strength and the amphibious capability it enjoyed through navy gunboats made any real defense of Florida's Atlantic and Gulf coasts all but impossible. A mobile defense provided the only real alternative in the face of possible Union thrusts inland.

Governor Milton did not support the creation of more mounted units for such a mobile defense, arguing that cavalry in Florida would be counter-productive. Events over-ruled the earnest executive, and men and horses were assembled to hold back the Unionists. Such units would not be effective, however, if they were not properly led. The cavalry raider was a very important part of Confederate military history, as they could move fast, strike hard, then fade away in the face of pursuit. Men like J.E.B. Stuart, Turner Ashby, Joseph Wheeler, John S. Mosby, and Nathan Bedford Forrest were tremendous assets to the South. Their missions tied down thousands of Union troops, disrupted communications and transportation, and destroyed millions of dollars worth of military property. Southern men followed such officers because they gave them adventure and victory over the hated foe. Florida's contribution to this elite group was John Jackson Dickison.

Dickison, raised in the South Carolina Lowcountry, moved to the rich lands of Marion County in 1856 to seek success as a planter. With the labor of his slaves Dickison soon prospered in Florida, as did so many of his fellow Carolinians, but the coming of civil war changed everything. In 1861 he organized a cavalry company among his Marion County neighbors but ended up soldiering for a time in the Marion Artillery. However, his planter status and prior service in the South Carolina state militia made an officer's commission almost a certainty for Dickison. In the summer of 1862 he took his place as commanding officer of Company H, Second Florida Cavalry Regiment.

Dickison's cavalry command averaged around 75 men, all from North and Central Florida. Good riders and better shots, these Floridians learned to live off the land and capture what they needed from the Yanks. Naturally they depended on the local civilian population for further supplies and vital information on enemy activity. In many ways their war resembled that of modern guerrillas of whom Chinese theorists Sun Tzu and Mao would have approved. In time their exploits became the stuff of legends and made them notorious among Federals in the state. "War Eagle" Dickison and his men blazed a trail from one end of the peninsula to the other by 1865.

Dickison's main area of operation was the St. Johns River valley, with his mission being to halt Union efforts to raid west of the river and disrupt Confederate efforts to gather supplies and move them northward. Soon Federal soldiers called the county west of the river "Dixieland" and knew that an ambush by swift rebel riders there was always a chance. Dickison's endeavors usually met with success as he knew the land and took great care in the planning of each mission. His troopers were always well briefed about their roles in any attack and had full confidence in his leadership. Camp Baldwin near Waldo served as their base camp when not out in the piney woods on patrol.

Probably the "War Eagle's" greatest success in the field was his capture on the St. Johns of the USS *Columbine* on May 23, 1864. In October of that same year Nathan Bedford Forrest's men managed the same feat of arms on the Tennessee River. Could the legendary cavalryman have been inspired to make such a bold attack by news of Dickison's triumph? Both leaders did believe that a small force could defeat a larger and more powerful one if it were audacious enough. Regardless of these victories Dickison's raiders helped maintain

*Here is the capture of the gunboat* Columbine *in 1864. (Taken from* Dickison and His Men.*)*

*Jacksonville is seen here during the Union occupation in 1864. A single Union sentry surveys the landscape for possible Confederate activity, ignoring the bustling scene below him. (National Archives.)*

the fragile strategic balance and military status quo in Florida and inspire pro-Confederates there to keep up the fight.

By the mid-point of the war in 1863 the Florida theater of war was a secondary one to both sides at best, and each concentrated resources elsewhere. Jacksonville was occupied yet again in March and subsequently evacuated by the end of the month, much to the dismay of eastern Florida Unionists. Federal troops also left the city of Pensacola during the same time in an effort to concentrate their forces around the military forts in the area. Other assorted skirmishes and naval raids on salt works paled in comparison to the fighting around Vicksburg, Charleston, and, by July, at Gettysburg. But forces were at work that would raise Florida from military obscurity, at least temporarily, and focus attention on the peninsula for a time. The end result would be Florida's largest Civil War battle, fought at an isolated place named Olustee.

The origins of the Olustee campaign can be traced to Union frustrations with the ongoing siege of Charleston. The overall commander before Charleston, Major General Quincy A. Gilmore, chafed at his men's lack of progress against the strongly defended city and ached for action somewhere. Gilmore concluded that a strike at north Florida just might check the flow of supplies to Charleston, and thereby hasten its fall. He pitched the idea to the Union army's general in chief, Henry W. Halleck, who received the plan with little enthusiasm. "Old Brains" Halleck did not want to waste troops acquiring more Southern territory of dubious strategic value and then be stuck garrisoning it. Gilmore assured his superior that a Florida strike could be made early in 1864 without any additional troops being sent to his department.

Ohioan Gilmore pressed Halleck with all the potential benefits his Florida campaign might accrue. Florida cotton, lumber, and naval stores could be seized and sent north to hungry consumers. Commissary stores being taken out of the state, no secret to Union officers who had read the famous White Circular, could be taken and rebel supply line to Georgia and South Carolina effectively cut. Gilmore also hinted at the possibility that a significant number of African-American males in Florida would flock to the colors and enlist in the Union army if given a chance. Lastly and sensitively, the general thought that the entire state of Florida might be reconstructed in time for the 1864 presidential election if the proposed operation were to succeed. Permission from the War Department in Washington to proceed was forthcoming.

The 1864 Florida campaign began with still another Federal landing in Jacksonville on February 7, and the war-ravished town fell into Yankee hands with slight resistance. Gunboats slipped past the city escorting troop-carrying vessels bound to take possession of Palatka and Picolata farther up the St. Johns. In short order Union troops began inching their way westward along the tracks of the Florida, Atlantic, and Gulf Railroad. The few Confederates in the area did little to stop this advance and retreated in the direction of Lake City. Union Brigadier General Truman A. Seymour, the commander on the ground, remained unsure of rebel intentions and whether he should lead his men to Lake City and perhaps Tallahassee beyond. His dispatches back to General Gilmore ran from grave concern for his position to jaunty confidence, though to date not much had come of his efforts.

*Brigadier General Truman Seymour, USA.*

Confederate leaders on the other hand had no doubt of the seriousness of the Yankee thrust into Florida. Senior commander General P.G.T. Beauregard felt the danger to his defense of Charleston posed by Seymour's men in north Florida, and moved to check it. Reinforcements under Georgian Albert H. Colquitt marched at the quick to join local forces under Florida General Joseph Finegan, gathering to stop the Yankees cold. Unaware of the enemy troops massing before him, Seymour ordered his roughly 5,000 men to move toward Lake City and westward to the Suwannee River if practical. Hopes of taking the state capital or much of anything else were dashed when the bluecoats ran into a strong Confederate position at Olustee Station on the rail line. These defenses were manned by roughly the same number of rebel soldiers as in Seymour's assaulting force.

At approximately 2:30 p.m. on February 20, 1864, Yankees and Southerners made contact at Olustee and a fierce battle ensued. A withering barrage of rifle and cannon fire decimated the advancing Federals, as did wooden splinters from pine trees shattered by artillery fire. Many of Seymour's troops had seen little or no action to date, and in the shriek of battle some men failed to do their duty. The entrenched Confederates poured on their fire, and cut huge gaps in the Federal lines as men fell dead or wounded. Inexperienced or incompetent officers froze at key moments and made command mistakes that only increased casualties among their men. By 6:30 p.m. the battered Union regiments broke contact and began a disorganized retreat in the direction of Jacksonville. Only the skillful rearguard action of the famous Fifty-Fourth Massachusetts Infantry and the First North Carolina, both African-American regiments, kept the withdrawal from becoming a bloody rout.

The defeated Union column did not stop till safely in the Jacksonville area, where it took stock after the setback. Seymour had lost some 1,861 battle casualties at Olustee and wrecked several of his regiments. Word filtering back that wounded African-American soldiers left behind during the retreat had been killed by angry rebels did nothing to ease the pain of failure. Large amounts of equipment had been lost, including 6 artillery pieces and 39 valuable horses. Countless amounts of weapons, accouterments, and ammunition also littered the line of retreat.

Olustee was a clear Confederate victory that raised spirits across the South after a bleak winter. Finegan contented himself gleaning all the abandoned military stores from the battlefield and dealing with the 946 casualties that his men had taken during the sharp engagement. The fact that Seymour's command contained several African-American regiments made the victory sweet for numbers of Confederates. One Georgia newspaper described the Unionists as walking "forty miles over the most barren land of the South, frightening the salamanders and the gophers, and getting a terrible thrashing. . . ."

The North greeted the news of Olustee with shock and anger, and many wanted explanations of why the operation had gone so badly and at such a high cost in lives. The luckless General Seymour was quickly transferred to the Army of the Potomac, and his superior Gilmore was happy to let the unfortunate affair fade away. The Northern press railed about the Lincoln Administration's political objectives that contributed to the Florida fiasco and that the president would pay for it at the polls in November. However the momentous events of the summer of 1864, primarily the advances of Grant and Sherman's armies, pushed Olustee out of the papers and out of Northern memories. The

*The Battle of Olustee, the largest and most costly Civil War battle fought in Florida, is depicted in a contemporary Union print by Louis Kurz.*

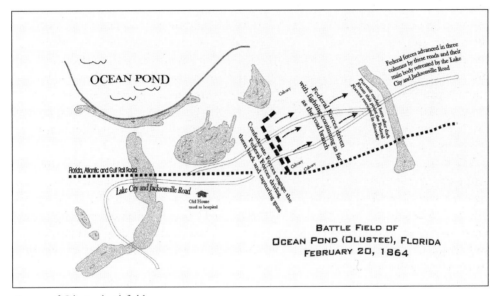

*A map of Olustee battlefield.*

outcome of Florida's greatest wartime combat led Union leaders to reduce troops levels on the peninsula and let it return to a sleepy secondary sector. That was just fine for the battered Union veterans of bloody Olustee. One of their number wrote with some bitterness, "the whole state of Florida is not worth half the suffering and anguish this battle has caused."

From Olustee till the end of the war, reduced Union forces engaged in relatively small raids or repelled rebel attacks on their bases and outposts. The Confederates rushed down to augment Finegan's men were also returned to more pressing fronts outside the state, so the stalemate continued as it did before. This is not to say that the men who marched or rode through the hot Florida sun or endured short rations and slow mails from home were not as important or significant as the men under Grant, Sherman, Lee, and Johnston

*Major General John Newton was the commander of Federal forces at the Battle of Natural Bridge. (National Archives.)*

battling it out in Virginia and Georgia that summer of 1864. At times they even played roles in the greater strategic scheme of the larger war.

General U.S. Grant, now the leader of all Union armies, yearned for sometime to capture Mobile and end its career as a blockade-runner's sanctuary. The naval battle of Mobile Bay on August 5 was a Union triumph and cut off Mobile's water access to the Gulf of Mexico. But the Gulf coast area beckoned to Union commanders, and raids originating in Pensacola struck neighboring Alabama and targets in the Florida Panhandle. Union Brigadier General Alexander S. Asboth commanded the military District of West Florida and was determined to strike the rebels at any opportunity. The fiery Asboth, a refugee from the failed 1848 Hungarian revolution, led a raiding force to distant Marianna in Jackson County in September and sacked the town. Marianna's defenders, mostly old men and boys, were unable to hold back Asboth's soldiers, though General Asboth himself was seriously wounded during the fighting.

In distant South Florida a similar type of war went on without relent, both sides knowing that any disruption of cattle gathering there might mean the difference between victory and defeat. A thorn in the side of Confederate Floridians was the Union base at old Fort Myers, which shielded Unionists and offered regular troops a base from which

*A map of the Battle of Natural Bridge and the proposed attack on Tallahassee.*

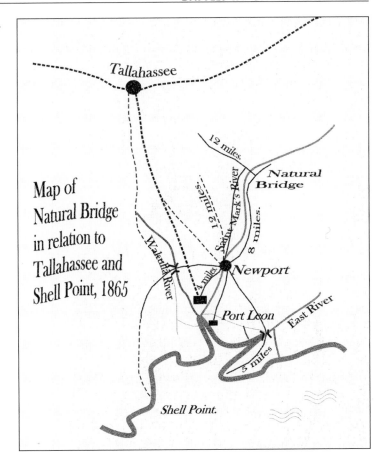

Map of Natural Bridge in relation to Tallahassee and Shell Point, 1865

Tallahassee

12 miles

Natural Bridge

Saint Mark's River

12 miles

8 miles

Wakulla River

3 miles

Newport

East River

Port Leon

5 miles

Shell Point.

to strike the cattle herds to the east. In February 1865 elements of the Cow Cavalry battalion, led by William Footman, moved to launch a surprise attack on the enemy fort. However the light cavalry found they were facing the strong defenses of Fort Myers, and bitterly broke off the attack. Morale remained low in the battalion as it rode back toward Tampa and their regular duties.

The dawning of 1865 brought a fourth year to the blood-spattered conflict raging in North America. Confederate supporters had little to be optimistic about as they watched the South's chances for independence fade away. Abraham Lincoln, now safely in the White House for another four-year term, remained determined to crushed the rebellion and re-unite all the states in one nation. Atlanta had fallen, and Sherman had marched from there to Savannah in a campaign designed to "make Georgia howl." By the spring of 1865 his armies rolled northward through the Carolinas brushing aside any rebel attempts to halt them. In Virginia, Lee's army endured another terribly hard, hungry winter at Petersburg but did not dare hope that Grant's bulldog grip on them would relax. As the climax of the national drama opened, Florida saw one last flurry of military activity.

The ever-tightening Union naval blockade pushed Federal officers to ensure that even smaller Confederate ports were closed to smugglers. St. Marks on the Gulf coast was one

141

such tempting target. Its close proximity to the state capital in Tallahassee offered the prospects of a successful raid to those brave enough to make it. General John Newton, the Federal commander of the District of Key West in early 1865, believed he could make an amphibious landing with the men at his disposal and not only destroy valuable rebel property but take Tallahassee as well. He organized a force including Second and Ninety-ninth United States Colored Troops Infantry Regiments as well as elements of the Unionist Second Florida Cavalry. They boarded transports at Key West and Cedar Key for the run up the coast to St. Marks.

On a fog-shrouded March 4, Newton's large 1,000-man strike force hit the beach and moved on St. Marks with all possible speed. The plan consisted of wrecking enemy property at the small community of Newport, then crossing the St. Marks River and striking the town and the railroad tracks connecting it with Tallahassee some 18 miles to the north. However, local defense forces thwarted their movement by burning the railroad bridge over the river and forcing the Yankees to trudge another 8 miles along the riverbank to another possible fording place. Here the river dipped underground for several hundred feet and created literally a natural bridge. Unfortunately for Newton it also created a natural "choke point" for defenders under the command of rebel General William Miller.

Miller led soldiers from the Second Florida Cavalry battalion, the local militia, and a cadet company from the West Florida Seminary (now Florida State University) in Tallahassee to hold the key spot at Natural Bridge and break up the enemy raid. On March 6, 1865, the Union forces attempted to force their way across the earthen bridge but found entrenched rebels putting up a deadly crossfire. Emboldened by their success, Miller's Confederates rushed at the Yankees in a counter-charge that quickly ground to a halt in the face of Union artillery fire. A disappointed Newton, realizing that any dreams of riding into Tallahassee in triumph were gone, ordered a retreat back to St. Marks and waiting friendly warships. Thus ended the battle of Natural Bridge; a Confederate victory at the cost of 3 killed and 28 wounded. Union casualties of all types numbered 148.

One senior Confederate official, W.K. Beard, praised the spirited defense of Natural Bridge as an example of what a determined people can do in the face of Yankees assaults. He believed that "while this spirit animates the southern people we have no fears of the Yankees. Let them do their worst." While such valiant statements uplifted Floridian's morale for a time, the win at Natural Bridge was only a small glimmer of light in the increasing darkness of impending Confederate defeat and destruction. The rest of March saw only setbacks and the crumbling of the rebel cause. By April, Richmond was evacuated and captured, and soon the fabled Army of Northern Virginia made its last forced march to Appomattox Court House and its rendezvous with history. Lee officially surrendered it to Grant there on April 9, 1865.

Even after Lee's capitulation the Civil War did indeed continue for several weeks in sections of the Confederacy not under direct Union control. General Sam Jones, the last rebel commander in Florida, issued a circular to his men on April 28 explaining what the surrender at Appomattox meant in the greater scope of the war. As the Army of Northern Virginia was scarcely two-thirds the size of the forces lost when Vicksburg surrendered in 1863, in Jones's view Lee's loss was not fatal to the Confederate ability to continue the fight for independence. As the war was far from over he begged his men "to stand firm

**HEADQ'RS, DIST. OF FLORIDA,**
Tallahassee, April 28th, 1865.

In view of the vague and uncertain reports which have reached us from Virginia, the Major General Commanding deems it proper to say frankly, that whilst he has no official information on the subject from the Head Quarters of the Army, circumstantial testimony induces the belief that we have suffered a serious reverse, but to what extent he is not informed. He believes the reports to be greatly exaggerated. But if the reports in their wildest form are true, the force recently surrendered in Virginia is scarcely more than two-thirds of that surrendered at Vicksburg, nearly two years since, and within the last three months we have probably received in our midst a greater number of men, exchanged prisoners, than was recently surrendered in Virginia.

We rallied from the disaster of Vicksburg, and with the aid of our exchanged veterans,

"We'll rally 'round the battle flag,
And rally once again;"

And if we are true to ourselves, and worthy of freedom, let us trust that the blessing of God will yet crown with success our efforts in a cause so noble. Only the skulkers and extortioners, the timid and craven, tremble and forget their manhood in the hour and presence of danger and adversity. They, to save their worthless lives and ill-gotten gains, may endeavor on the news to increase the feeling of despondency and induce others, better and braver than themselves, to relax their efforts and neglect their duty. Spurn all such from you as your worst enemies.

There are now the strongest reasons for standing firm and true to our colors, maintaining discipline and gathering and concentrating our strength. We have official information that an armistice has been agreed upon pending negotiations between the two governments for peace. In the mean time, it is not only the imperative duty, but to the interest of every man in the Confederacy, to stand firm and true and present a bold and defiant front to our enemies. Such a course will strengthen our government and aid in securing an honorable peace. A contrary course may embolden our enemies to demand terms that we cannot accept with honor.

I confidently rely on the troops in this District to stand loyally and truly to their colors, and await patiently the result of negotiations, in the firm conviction that our honor has not been tarnished by General Robert E. Lee, and that our government will never accept dishonorable terms.

SAM JONES,
Major General.

*Major General Sam Jones, commander of the District of Florida in 1865, issued this circular following the news of Lee's surrender in Virginia. (Florida State Archives.)*

and true and present a bold and defiant front to our enemies. Such a course will strengthen our government and aid in securing an honorable peace." Few believed Jones's incredibly optimistic picture, and all looked forward to the opportunity to lay down their arms, swear the required oath of allegiance to the Union, and return to civilian life.

Triumphant Union troops did finally march into Tallahassee on May 10, 1865, and joined in the paroling of all remaining Confederate units in Florida. They were also on the lookout for fleeing rebel leaders like Judah P. Benjamin and John C. Breckinridge, said to be fleeing down the Florida peninsula. In Tallahassee, Brigadier General Edward McCook, of the "fighting McCooks of Ohio," oversaw local forces and made sure that a large Stars and Stripes banner flew once again over the city. Local clergy were also informed that in their Sabbath prayers the President of the United States should once again be included whether they cared to or not. The war was indeed over.

While Florida was spared the carnage of battles like Fredericksburg or Chickamauga, it saw its own type of Civil War combat that was just as real and deadly to those involved as any other in the conflict. Rifles cracked and cannons blasted out explosive charges that often meant painful death or dismemberment to the unlucky. Raids, skirmishes, and pitched battles, albeit on a small scale, rocked the peninsula from Pensacola to Fort Myers and Jacksonville to Tampa Bay. Pro-Confederate Floridians fended off Union attacks whether they were raids, ambushes laid by J.J. Dickison's command, or set piece engagements like Olustee or Natural Bridge. Ironically, the two largest fights in Civil War Florida were rebel victories, and the capital never fell to Yankee forces during the entire War between the States. Union forces, many of them African Americans, often met with frustration on the Florida peninsula and never accomplished what they hoped to there. However, these Billy Yanks fought with valor and bravery for their cause in what was for them an exotic tropical climate. In the end Confederate Florida died with the rest of the Confederate states and moved with uncertainty into the post-war world.

# 10. Florida in the Reconstruction Era

When the guns of the Civil War finally ceased firing in the summer of 1865, the United States faced the unprecedented challenge of re-uniting itself after four bloody years of civil warfare. Nowhere in the Constitution or in American governmental memory were there any guidelines for such action, and leaders offered many differing views about who should do it and how it should be done. The nation would have to proceed without its greatest political leader, as Abraham Lincoln was already dead from an assassin's bullet. The new president, Andrew Johnson of Tennessee, inherited the problem and went into it with many of the perceptions of his antebellum yeoman Southern background. Also, the American people, North and South, would have to come to terms with the death of chattel slavery and the elevation of African Americans to the full promise of American life.

Florida began the post-war era without a chief executive, as Governor Milton had taken his own life in the wake of Confederate defeat. Acting Governor Abraham K. Allison assumed the office and began creating a post-Confederate state government by calling for a meeting of the General Assembly in June 1865. However, Union General Edward McCook, under order from the War Department in Washington, suspended Allison's efforts and declared martial law throughout the state on May 22. Federal troops, many of them African-American units, fanned out across the state to garrison principal towns and see that laws and military orders from Tallahassee were enforced. At times their presence only fueled tensions, as many Floridians had not accepted the war's outcome and the ending of racial slavery. They certainly were not ready for the sight of black troopers marching through their towns and demanding equal rights and treatment.

The new administration of Andrew Johnson in Washington did move to re-start some sort of civil life for Florida with the appointment of Key West's William Marvin as acting governor. Marvin's pro-Unionist positions and his credentials as a Southerner helped when he called for a new constitutional convention in October 1865. The Union military in the state contributed logistically to the election of delegates, which included all eligible white voters who had taken the oath of allegiance to the Federal government. The canvass

LEFT: *Brigadier General Edward McCook led Federal troops occupying Florida's capital on May 10, 1865. (Tebeau-Field Library of Florida History.)*
RIGHT: *Acting Governor Abraham K. Allison assumed the chief executive's office following the suicide of Governor John Milton on April 1, 1865. (Florida State Archives.)*

all but ignored the newly freed African Americans in the state but saw several well-known ex-Confederates returning to the state capital as elected officials.

While the 1865 state convention ratified, albeit without enthusiasm, the Thirteenth Amendment banning slavery forever and repealed the 1861 Ordinance of Secession, it did practically nothing to recognize the new paradigm in race relations. In fact Florida followed the example of its neighboring states and enacted a series of laws known as "black codes" based on pre-war slave laws. These were designed to make certain that blacks, despite the war, would remain second-class non-citizens. Some of the new statues, like the new vagrancy laws, were much harsher than in antebellum times and created a new serf-like status for many former slaves. The convention made plans to elect a new delegation from Florida to the United States Congress, but many of them were formerly Confederate supporters. It seemed to many observers that Florida and the rest of the ex-Confederate South were busy winning the peace and undermining the Union victory in the late conflict.

President Johnson, unfortunately, never measured up to Lincoln's political abilities and never challenged his home region to go beyond its current racial views. By the fall of 1865 Congress had refused to seat new members from the former rebel states and demanded investigations and more protection for former slaves. The duel over control of Reconstruction went on into 1866 when the House and the Senate passed over Johnson's

*Andrew Johnson, vice president from Tennessee, assumed the presidency of the United States following the assassination of Abraham Lincoln in April 1865.*

veto, the first such override in American history, of a civil rights act to shield those facing violence and overt discrimination. Congress also extended the life of a wartime agency, the Bureau of Refugees, Freedmen, and Abandoned Lands, so that it might continue its needed work in the South. The U.S. Army was pressed to be more aggressive in going after vigilante groups like the newly formed Ku Klux Klan. Despite Johnson's considerable political exertions, Congress eventually took control of the entire rehabilitation program from the President with the passage of the First Reconstruction Act on March 21, 1867. It would be followed by two more by July, and a new era came south of the Mason-Dixon Line.

Congress pressed the army into service as the chief Reconstruction agency, hence giving it its first taste of nation-building at home. By early April 1867 this became reality in Florida as the civilian government in Tallahassee came under military orders from a

147

commanding officer, Colonel John T. Sprague. The Freedmen's Bureau came under direct military protection and coordinated its activities with the military. This was accomplished with little trouble, as many Freedmen's Bureau agents were ex-Union army officers. The bureau's head in Florida was one such Union veteran, Thomas W. Osborn, and he immediately pushed former slaves to return to the plantations and sign labor contracts with the owners to get the state's agricultural economy going again. On the other hand, under Osborn the bureau set up schools and clinics for those in need and offered legal advice to ex-slaves grappling with freedom's problems. The African-American community in Florida, often with nothing but liberty and the clothes on their backs, rose to the task of becoming free, productive citizens and building new lives for themselves and the generations to come.

New economic patterns led naturally to new political ones. Under the new Reconstruction Acts and the proposed Fourteenth Amendment, adult black males over the age of 21 would be registered to vote across the old Confederacy. Any state that balked at this registration edict would find itself denied full admission to Congress and to the rest of the United States. As the voting roles filled with new names, the Republican Party opted to take advantage of the situation and expand its base into the South. New voters were lobbied to join the grand new party and sign up for groups like the Lincoln Brotherhood and the Loyal League of America. Both of these organizations were adjuncts of the national Republican organization. In Florida, to the horror of old Democrats, the new Republicans grew by leaps and bounds and enjoyed the umbrella of military protection. Membership included many newcomers from the North who would have to endure the tag "carpetbagger." These people, contrary to popular belief, came south for the most part with capital to invest and leadership experience to share and not to take advantage of defeated Southerners. Native Floridians of a Unionist bent, nicknamed "scalawags" by their political enemies, joined the new party as well. Though thoroughly dominated by whites, Florida's new Republican Party was definitely "black and tan" in make-up and determined to make serious changes in the state. Obviously, old guard Conservative Democrats disliked what they saw and pledged to stop this revolution and return things to what in their view was the rightful order of things.

In November 1867 another election took place that saw the participation of the new bi-racial Florida electorate. While Republicans—to the surprise of no one—dominated at the polls, only 18 black delegates were selected out of 43 in total. Despite this lack of numbers, black Floridians were indeed thrilled to break racial barriers and sit in Tallahassee as certified legislators. A new constitution, finished in 1868, emerged in the midst of internal bickering among various factions inside the new party, and it proved to be the most progressive in the state's history to that time. Harrison Reed, formerly from Wisconsin and an ex-Treasury Department agent, won the governorship. The convention also picked a new slate of Congressional office-holders, including men like Charles H. Hamilton of Marianna, per the terms of the Reconstruction Acts.

Republican Reed took the oath of office on June 8, 1868, and by July 4, full civilian government returned to Florida from military hands. Congress had already acted by placing the peninsula state in an omnibus bill that re-admitted it to the Union along with four other ex-Confederate states on June 25. The Reed years, however, would be far from

*Josiah Thomas Walls was a state senator in Florida and became the first African American from the state to serve in the U.S. House of Representatives. (Florida State Archives.)*

pacific as the forces of conservative reaction organized and moved to halt what they considered the "evils" of Reconstruction. They grew in strength and in boldness, and the few regular troops in the state had a difficult time finding these new night raiders much less capturing them. Many rural Florida counties suffered from acts of violence against Republicans of both colors, and local law enforcement seemed powerless to stop it. Army troops were not all that effective as they were mostly infantry units trying to capture mounted vigilantes, as the cavalry regiments were deployed on the Great Plains by the late 1860s. Thus, robed nightriders wreaked havoc among the black community and targeted landowners in particular for their terrorism.

The reign of hate peaked in Jackson County in 1869 with a coordinated campaign against the Republican Party's black and white leadership. At least 17 murders took place there by "person or persons unknown." The state government was helpless, and Governor Reed feared that calling out the newly re-formed biracial militia against these criminals might unleash an even more horrible race war. By the 1870s Republican activity in Jackson County stood at near zero, and in many other Middle Florida counties, any such political work was very dangerous it not suicidal.

Even in the face of such obvious threats, the "black and tans" strove to create a new and better Florida. Many new African-American leaders served in positions of power and responsibility that they did not dream of before 1865. One such man was Josiah T. Walls, a former Union soldier and veteran of the Florida legislature. In 1870 he became the first black Floridian to sit in the U.S. House of Representatives as a member. Walls even managed, ironically, to purchase the plantation of a former Confederate general during his six years in Congress. Another prominent African-American politician, Jonathan Gibbs, had the distinction of being one of the best-educated solons in Florida due to his Ivy League schooling. He ended up as the highest-ranking black state official during Reconstruction by serving as secretary of state from 1868 to 1872. Gibbs went from that position to the complicated and frustrating task of being the state superintendent of public education. Gibbs struggled hard to create a public school system in Florida with few resources and much hostility from people.

Nationally, reconstructing the South remained a nagging issue even after Andrew Johnson's near removal from office after his impeachment and Senate trial in 1868. His successor in the White House, savior of the Union turned Republican politico Ulysses S. Grant, called for a return to normalcy with his 1868 campaign slogan "Let Us Have Peace." A far less able political leader than general, Grant let Reconstruction slide down from the top of national priorities, except when he used troops to beef up the anti-Ku Klux

*Jonathan Gibbs was Florida's secretary of state and superintendent of public instruction during the Reconstruction period. (Florida State Archives.)*

Klan work of the new Enforcement Acts in the early 1870s. Such efforts did curtail Klan activities in many parts of the South.

The issues of the war across the North were cooling in general, and new challenges like the winning of the trans-Mississippi West, the rise of industry, and the growth of urban America took their place. In fact many Northerners grew tired of the perennial troubles coming from the Southern states, and more than a few desired the U.S. government get out of the business altogether. Support for the freedmen waned despite such things as the Enforcement Acts and the ratification of the Fifteenth Amendment in 1870, which gave adult black males the constitutional right to vote. Another factor was the passing of the abolitionist generation either in death or disillusionment as America entered what author Mark Twain labeled the Gilded Age.

In sunny Florida the beginnings of a post-war economic boomlet stumbled over the on-going political squabbles. Wealthy Northerners with vision and money looked to Florida for investment opportunities and wanted a stable state government with which to do business. This was especially true with investors thinking of expanding the amount of railroad track running through the peninsula. With Republicans at war with each other and conservative Democrats in the wings biding their time, the state's political landscape was far from orderly. Governor Reed survived numerous impeachment efforts from his enemies and finally left office discredited. In the 1872 election, Republicans tapped Ossian

*William D. Bloxham. (Florida State Archives.)*

B. Hart as a hopeful replacement for Reed. Hart was a native Floridian with strong Unionist ties; he was able to defeat the serious challenge from conservative Democrat William D. Bloxham and win the governorship. However, any promise that Hart may have had was short-lived, as he died in office in 1874.

Lieutenant Governor Marcellus L. Stearns, an ex-Freedmen's Bureau agent, took over and labored to expand his power base for the next election. Unfortunately, Stearns decided to do this by jettisoning the black Republicans in favor of an all-white party. In a rising atmosphere of tension and race violence Floridians waited for 1876 to see if the Republicans could hold on to power in the face of conservative Democrats "bulldozer" tactics or if they would lose and Florida could be "redeemed" by the conservatives.

In the centennial year 1876 the nation stood transfixed by the impending presidential election. President Grant, though willing to run a third time, was damaged goods due to the almost nonstop series of scandals rocking his eight years in office. The Republican convention that year passed over many of its brighter stars for the "available" Governor Rutherford B. Hayes of Ohio. Hayes was little known but had angered no faction and had a very good Civil War battle record. The Democrats, still reeling from the political tumults of the 1860s and smelling victory, nominated New York Governor Samuel J. Tilden. Tilden had a reputation as a reformer and a foe of the infamous Tweed Ring. While both men were solid, capable men, neither one could ever boast of being a charismatic leader. Both parties geared up for what turned out to be one of the most controversial elections in American history.

Nationwide Republicans were worried that Tilden just might win the Presidency, but in the South they felt fear bordering on panic. The Florida Republican party backed away from its bi-racial roots by November 1876 when it refused to even re-nominate Representative Josiah T. Walls for another term in Congress and put together an all-white ticket. Most Florida citizens focused on the key local contests and cared little which of the two Yankees running moved into the White House in 1877. But as the votes were tabulated Florida found itself catapulted into the national spotlight

By Election Day, 1876, only three Southern states, South Carolina, Louisiana, and Florida, remained under Republican control. All the other former Confederate states had been "redeemed" by the Democrats and were safely in the Tilden column. Vigilante violence targeted at African Americans, Northern "carpetbaggers," and native "scalawags," few of whom dared appear at the polls, kept them there. The three unredeemed states also saw voter intimidation and outright fraud on a large scale, and no clear winner could be declared in any of them. Alert members of the Hayes camp quickly saw that if Hayes could somehow take the electoral votes of all three contested Southern states he could edge Tilden out of the Presidency by a 185 to 184 total. Both sides rushed forces to the states in question and prepared to battle it out for the winning tally.

Less than 50,000 Floridians voted in 1876, a depressed figure that can be tied to threats and hostility against potential voters. But as these ballots were sorted and counted it appeared that only a few hundred votes separated the two presidential candidates. Each side hurled accusations at each other of tampering with the counting or adding a few votes after the polls closed. As the sparks flew Tallahassee filled with representatives from the national parties who were there to ensure that their candidate received his fair share of the

*Rutherford B. Hayes of Ohio.*

*Samuel J. Tilden of New York.*

votes cast. In this blizzard of charges and counter-charges state officials finally certified that Hayes garnered 23,843 votes to Tilden's 22,919 and therefore the Ohioan had taken Florida's electoral votes. The state supreme court had to certify the election of Democrat George F. Drew as Florida's next chief executive. Governor Stearns reluctantly surrendered his office under the threat of gunfire in the streets of Tallahassee on January 2, 1877.

Just who the next President of the United States would be was far less clear. Democrats in Florida, not surprisingly, demanded a recount and sent a certification of Tilden's victory in the state to Congress. But the House and the Senate opted to decide such issues though a special election commission with eight Republicans and seven Democrats charged with finding the true winner. The commission settled the Florida claims and those of the other states in question with a strict party vote of eight to seven for Hayes. He was subsequently declared the winner, though the President-elect entered office under a cloud and had to endure names such as "Eight to Seven Hayes," or "Rutherfraud." Consequently Hayes only served one term as President and then faded into obscurity. Never before had Florida played such a pivotal role in a national election, and it proved not to be the last time.

Historians record that one of the reasons that Hayes emerged victorious in 1877 was a series of assurances his supporters gave in return for Southern electoral votes. These included the withdrawal of regular troops from South Carolina, Louisiana, and Florida, which meant an effective end to Federal government involvement in Reconstruction. If a "deal" did exist in 1877, Hayes lived up to it and removed the soldiers from the South and watched from the sidelines as the Republican governments in each fell one by one. In Florida the party suffered a near fatal blow as its black-white coalition came undone. By the dawning of the 20th century Florida was solidly under Democratic control with only a few politically impotent pockets of Republicans scattered around the peninsula.

Another casualty of the end of Reconstruction in Florida was the state's African-American community. The bright promises of 1867 had faded by 1877 as political power waned and then political participation all but halted. By 1900 the white-dominated state government instituted a series of laws that created a segregated Florida and then made certain that separate was not equal. These "Jim Crow" laws became a hard reality that left a legacy of discrimination that Florida would have to labor hard to overcome. Anyone of African-American descent who resisted this concerted effort against their people faced the all too common horror of the lynch law in much of the state.

Though Reconstruction ended on a dour note with promises unkept and alliances denied, the Civil War and its offspring created the tools for a better world for all Floridians. The Thirteenth, Fourteenth, and Fifteenth Amendments remained part of the Constitution and, by the post–World War II era, would be re-discovered by a new generation of legal minds and used to chip away at the Jim Crow system in all areas of society. The memories of brave black leaders of Reconstruction Florida served as an inspiration for their descendents who took up the fight in the 1950s and 1960s. Then the assurance of what Lincoln called "a new birth of freedom" would be fulfilled in Florida and the rest of the American nation.

# EPILOGUE
## THE CONTROVERSY CONTINUES

Perhaps no other episode in American history has had a greater impact on the United States than the War between the States, most often referred to in shorthand as the "Civil War." Even today, Americans are dealing with the ramifications of that war while still dealing with its root causes. Legislatures in the various capitals of the states that made up the Confederate States of America wrangle with the questions of what symbols of that great epic are to be preserved and how they are to be displayed in public.

Patriotic groups, such as the Sons of Confederate Veterans, demand the right to have the Confederate battle flag displayed on public buildings and in public ceremonies, while African-American and human rights groups are just as adamant in their demands that the flag be banned from all but the most restrictive uses in museums and at historical sites. Supporters of the right to display the symbols of the Confederacy argue that the war was primarily an economic and political dispute that had little to do with slavery. Some even point out that from an economic standpoint, slavery was a dying institution. The war came, they continue, when conflicts over the rights of individuals and states versus those of the national government could no longer be resolved through debate and compromise. Thus, the war represented a confrontation between honorable men who differed on essential questions of political theory, whose participants deserve to be honored for their patriotism, bravery, and commitment to principle. They conclude with the argument that the war, when it came, was the result of Northern aggression, not Southern desire.

For African Americans, these arguments are but cleverly reasoned attempts to divert attention from the odious realities of slavery. Southern society and economic prosperity was based solely on the exploitation of Negro slaves, they argue, and the war was simply a vain attempt by white Southerners to preserve this racist and inhumane system. Without slavery, there would have been no distinctive South, no planter class, and no reason for radical, divisive political ideas. The South owed its very existence to slavery, the argument continues, and this should be the sole focus of any historical treatment of the war.

The United States Congress and state legislatures are periodically pressed by African-American leaders to establish a program of compensation for the descendants of former slaves as a means of creating economic equity in American society. Such leaders hold both the national and state governments historically accountable in creating and legitimizing the institution of slavery and thus liable for the misery, horrors, and deprivation that occurred. Only some form of restitution can compensate in part for the travails of slaves and their descendants. Few national political leaders and even fewer state politicians subscribe to this idea. Nevertheless, the idea of compensation surfaces again and again.

Many of the current problems that arise over the question of the Civil War spring more from the activities of Southern political leaders after the war than the war itself. Determined to continue white control of the South, politicians mobilized economic, social, and political institutions to exclude African Americans from participation in the Southern mainstream. Discriminatory laws, the Jim Crow system, and extralegal organizations, such as the Ku Klux Klan and Knights of the White Camellia, were merely parts of a larger arsenal of weapons used to repress former slaves and their progeny. The fact that many former Confederates assumed leadership roles in these efforts to exclude and exploit African Americans gave credence to the argument that the South was still fighting the war it had lost on the battlefields. The national acceptance of the Ku Klux Klan in the 1920s and the continuing refusal of most Americans to grant equal status to blacks until the upheavals of the 1960s further exacerbated race relations in the United States. The wholesale adoption of Confederate symbols by white extremists, who continue to flaunt these symbols and to define them solely in terms of race hatred, pollutes the issue to such a degree that any rational discussion of the Confederacy and its legacy in the public arena is not possible.

Yet despite all of the rhetoric and emotion involved in such a discussion, failure to explore this defining moment in American history with as much thoroughness as possible would be to ignore an essential element in understanding the American mind. Only by examining the Civil War in its totality is it possible to acquire a complete picture of what the United States was, what it is, and where it might go.

Robert A. Taylor
Nick Wynne
May 4, 2001

# SELECTED BIBLIOGRAPHY

Blakey, Arch Frederic, Ann Smith Lainhart, and Winston Bryant Stephens Jr. *Rose Cottage Chronicles: Civil War Letters of the Bryant-Stephens Families of North Florida*. Gainesville: University Press of Florida, 1998.

Boggess, Francis C.M. *A Veteran of Four Wars*. Arcadia, FL: Champion Press, 1900.

Brown, Canter, Jr. *Tampa in Civil War and Reconstruction*. Tampa: University of Tampa Press, 2000.

———. "The Civil War, 1861–1865." In *The New History of Florida*. ed. Michael Gannon. Gainesville: University Press of Florida, 1996.

Buker, George E. *Blockaders, Refugees, and Contrabands: Civil War on Florida's Gulf Coast*. Tuscaloosa: University of Alabama Press, 1993.

Cleveland, Mary Ann. "Florida Women During the Civil War." In *Florida Decades: A Sesquicentennial History 1845–1955*. eds. James J. Horgan and Lewis N. Wynne. St. Leo, FL: St. Leo College Press, 1995.

Coles, David J. " 'Far from Fields of Glory': Military Operations in Florida During the Civil War, 1864–1865." Ph.D. dissertation, Florida State University, 1996.

———. " 'A Fight, a Licking, and a Footrace': The 1864 Florida Campaign and the Battle of Olustee." Master's thesis, Florida State University, 1985.

Davis, William W. *The Civil War and Reconstruction in Florida*. New York: Columbia University Press, 1913.

Dickison, John J. "Military History of Florida." In *Confederate Military History*. ed. Clement Evans. 12 vols. Atlanta: Confederate Publishing Company, 1898.

Dickison, Mary E. *Dickison and His Men, Reminiscences of the War in Florida 1890*. ed. Samuel Proctor. Gainesville: University of Florida Press, 1962.

Dillion, Rodney E. Jr. "The Civil War in South Florida." Master's thesis, University of Florida, 1980.

Dodd, Dorothy. "Florida in the Civil War, 1861–1865." In *Florida Handbook 1961-1962*. ed. Allen Morris. Tallahassee: Peninsula Publishing, 1961.

Gannon, Michael. *Rebel Bishop: The Life and Era of Augustin Verot*. Milwaukee: The Bruce Publishing Company, 1964.

Itkin, Stanley L. "Operations of the East Gulf Blockade Squadron in the Blockade of Florida, 1862–1865." Master's thesis, Florida State University, 1962.

Johns, John E. *Florida During the Civil War*. Gainesville: University of Florida Press, 1963.

Loderhouse, Gary. *Far, Far from Home: The Ninth Florida Regiment in the Confederate Army*. Carmel, IN: Guild Press, 1999.

Lonn, Ella. *Salt as a Factor in the Confederacy*. Tuscaloosa: University of Alabama Press Edition, 1965.

Martin, Richard A., and Daniel L. Schafer. *Jacksonville's Ordeal by Fire: A Civil War History*. Jacksonville, FL: Florida Publishing Company, 1984.

Nulty, William H. *Confederate Florida: The Road to Olustee*. Tuscaloosa: University of Alabama Press, 1990.

Pearce, George F. *Pensacola During the Civil War: A Thorn in the Side of the Confederacy*. Gainesville: University Press of Florida, 2000.

Reiger, John F. "Anti-War and Pro-Union Sentiment in Confederate Florida." Master's thesis, University of Florida, 1966.

Revels, Tracy J. "Grander in Her Daughters: Florida's Women During the Civil War." *Florida Historical Quarterly* 77 (Winter 1999): 261–282.

Richardson, Joe M. *The Negro in the Reconstruction of Florida, 1865–1877*. Tallahassee: Florida State University Press, 1965.

Rivers, Larry E. *Slavery in Florida: Territorial Days to Emancipation*. Gainesville: University Press of Florida, 2000.

Schmidt, Lewis G. *The Civil War in Florida*. 4 vols. Allentown, PA: Lewis G. Schmidt, 1989.

Shofner, Jerrell H. *Nor Is It Over Yet: Florida in the Era of Reconstruction 1865–1877*. Gainesville: University of Florida Press, 1974.

Taylor, Robert A. "Unforgotten Threat: Florida Seminoles in the Civil War." *Florida Historical Quarterly* 69 (January 1991): 300–314.

———. *Rebel Storehouse: Florida in the Confederate Economy*. Tuscaloosa: University of Alabama Press, 1995.

Tebeau, Charlton W., and William Marina. *A History of Florida*. Third ed. Coral Gables, FL: University of Miami Press, 1999.

Trudeau, Noah Andre. *Like Men of War: Black Troops in the Civil War*. Boston: Little, Brown, 1998.

Urbach, Jon L. "An Appraisal of the Florida Secession Movement, 1859–1861." Master's thesis, Florida State University, 1972.

# INDEX